Student Study Guide
to Accompany

Social Work Research and Evaluation

Quantitative and Qualitative Approaches

Sixth Edition

Yvonne A. Unrau
Illinois State University

Judy Krysik
University of Denver

Richard M. Grinnell, Jr.
Illinois State University

Introduction

THIS STUDY GUIDE is to be used as an inexpensive supplement to Grinnell's sixth edition of *Social Work Research and Evaluation: Quantitative and Qualitative Approaches* (F.E. Peacock Publishers, 2001). As in the Grinnell text, its major goal is to aid your understanding of basic research methodology and its applications to social work problems.

ORGANIZATION

To accomplish this goal, the *Guide* is organized into two parts: (1) exercises, and (2) sample research studies.

Part I: Exercises

Part I contains 25 exercises that correspond directly to the 25 chapters in the 2001 Grinnell text. The exercises are intended to provide you with the opportunity to apply the basic concepts presented in the text to actual social work research studies contained in Part II.

To complement a variety of students' learning styles, three types of exercises are provided (i.e., self-study, group, and library). The self-study exercises require an individual, in-depth examination of each chapter. The group exercises facilitate class and group discussion. The library exercises encourage exploration of additional literature in an effort to strengthen your information retrieval skills.

The exercises are presented at varying levels of abstraction and require your creative and thoughtful input. For each set of exercises, you will be required to refer to a sample research study contained in Part II in the *Guide*.

Part II: Sample Research Studies

Part II contains seven (A–G) real-life social work research studies that provide concrete examples of how the research concepts described in the Grinnell text can be used in actual social work research studies.

THE *GUIDE* CAN BE EASILY MODIFIED

In an effort to acknowledge individual preferences of research instructors and students alike, this *Guide* can be modified in three ways:

1. Additional exercises (self-study, group, and library) can be formulated in addition to the ones that are currently contained in Part I.
2. Additional sample research studies can be used to supplement the ones that are currently contained in Part II.
3. A different sample research study can be used rather than the one that is presently required for an individual chapter. For example, it may be preferable for students to read Research Study B to correspond with Chapter 1 rather than Research Study C, which is now required in this *Guide*.

All in all, the flexibility of this *Guide* is limited to the imagination of the research instructor and/or student. Your creative use of this *Guide* is encouraged.

RECOMMENDED PROCEDURE TO COMPLETE THE EXERCISES

You will get the most benefit from this *Guide* if you follow a five-step procedure:

1. Read the set of exercises that corresponds to the specific chapter in the text. As you read the exercises make a preliminary mental note of the key terms, concepts, and themes. Highlight these by underlining them in the exercises.
2. Note the sample research study that you will have to read in order to complete the assigned exercises. If a different research study is assigned by your instructor, make sure to obtain a copy before completing the exercises.
3. Read the assigned chapter in the text, paying particular attention to the terms and concepts you previously identified when you perused the exercises in Step 1.
4. Read the sample research study referred to in the exercises or assigned by your research instructor. Pay special attention to the corresponding terms and concepts contained in the study.
5. Answer each question by combining your understanding of the material in the chapter and its application demonstrated in the research study.

ACKNOWLEDGMENTS

Research Study A: Flowers, J.V., & Booarem, C.D. (1990). Four studies toward an empirical foundation for group therapy. *Advances in Group Work Research, 5,* 105-121. (Used with permission, Haworth Press)

Research Study B: Moran, J.R. (1990). Social work education and students' humanistic attitudes. *Journal of Social Work Education, 25,* 13-19. (Used with permission, Council on Social Work Education)

Research Study C: Stephens, M.W., Grinnell, R.M., Jr., & Krysik, J.L. (1988). Victims of child sexual abuse: A research note. *Journal of Child Care, 3,* 65-76. (Used with permission, University of Calgary Press)

Research Study E: LeCroy, C.W., & Goodwin, C.C. (1988). New directions in teaching social work methods: A content analysis. *Journal of Social Work Education, 24,* 43-49. (Used with permission, Council on Social Work Education)

Research Studies D, F, G: Used with permission from the authors.

A FINAL WORD

The field of research in our profession is continuing to grow and develop. We believe this *Guide* will contribute to that growth. A seventh edition is anticipated, and suggestions for it are more than welcome. Please send your comments directly to:

Richard M. Grinnell, Jr.
Professor and Director
School of Social Work
Illinois State University
Normal, Illinois 61790- 4650

P a r t   I

Exercises

C h a p t e r   1

Introduction to Research

CHAPTER OUTLINE

SELF-STUDY EXERCISES

1. Before you entered your social work program and before you read the chapter, how did you think our profession obtained its knowledge base?

2. After reading the chapter, discuss in detail the various ways our profession obtains its knowledge base. Compare and contrast your answer to your response in Question 1. Do you feel Study C contributed to our knowledge base? If so, why? If not, why not?

3. List and discuss the reasons why we should never exclusively rely on our intuitions when making practice decisions. When is it necessary to make practice decisions based solely on intuition? Explain and discuss in detail using a social work example in your discussion.

4. What is "the research method?" How is this "method of knowing" more "objective" than the other ways of knowing? What method of knowing did Study C use? Discuss in detail. Discuss how the authors of Study C could have used the other four ways of knowing to address the same research question. Be specific in your answer. Provide specific hypothetical examples in your discussion.

5. List and discuss in detail the basic steps that the research method uses to obtain knowledge in our profession. Provide a social work example throughout your response. In relation to Study C, discuss how the authors must have used the basic steps contained within the research method.

6. List and briefly discuss the two complementary research approaches that are used within the research method way of knowing. Discuss in detail how Study C could have used the other research approach to answer the same research question.

7. Define the word *research* in your own words. How does your definition differ from the one provided in the chapter? What are the similarities and the differences between the two definitions? Discuss in detail.

8. List and discuss the two main goals of social work research studies. Provide a social work example in your discussion. Was Study C a pure or an applied research study? Justify your response.

10. What is the general research problem area in Study C? Why is it important to clearly define the problem area before embarking on a research study?

11. In your opinion, what other related research question could have been the focus of Study C? What factors motivated the development of *your* research question? Discuss in detail.

12. What role do you believe applied research plays in the social work profession? Discuss the similarities and the differences between applied and pure research using Study C as an example.

13. List and discuss in detail the three research roles social workers can take to generate knowledge for our profession. Relate your discussion to Study C.

14. Discuss how the integration of social work practice with social work research (social work practitioner/researcher) could enhance the development of our profession. Use the points as outlined in the chapter to justify your discussion and relate your response to Study C.

15. In your opinion, were the three social work research roles as outlined in the chapter integrated in Study C? Why, or why not? Use the points as outlined in the chapter to justify your discussion.

16. Read Box 1.1. What are your initial thoughts on the CSWE requiring research content to be taught at the undergraduate and graduate levels? Do you think the Council should require more or less research content to be taught in your school? If so, why. If not, why not?

17. Read Box 1.2. What are your initial thoughts on the NASW requiring its members to know research and evaluation content? Provide an example of each bullet point contained in Box 1.2 of how you believe each bullet point could be incorporated into your practice when you graduate.

18. Read Box 1.3. How could Madame *X* use the research method to evaluate her effectiveness? Be very concrete.

GROUP EXERCISES

1. In groups of four, discuss the possible problems you feel could surface between social work researchers and social work practitioners. Discuss how the research method of knowing—*one* of the ways of knowing—can be used to highlight the similarities rather than the differences between the two. How can the integration of the three research roles assist in diminishing potential problems? What other solutions can your group suggest to bridge the gap? Present your

findings, in point form, to your entire class. What are the various opinions of your group in reference to having to take a research course?

2. In groups of four, agree on one social work–related problem area (and a specific research question) and briefly discuss how each one of the ways of knowing could be used to answer the research question. What is the overall goal of your study? Present your findings to the entire class.

3. *A Hard Question.* At this very beginning point in your social work research course, and after reading Box 1.5, in groups of four, discuss the various cultural factors that you feel need to be taken into account when doing any social work research study. Do you feel any of these factors are different for doing a qualitative study verses a quantitative one? an applied study verses a pure one? Discuss in detail and provide one common social work example in your discussion. Report back to the entire class what your group found.

4. *A Very Hard Question.* At this very beginning point in your social work research course, and in groups of four, design a qualitative research study that proposes to answer a social work–related research question of your choice. With the same research question, design a quantitative research study. Compare the advantages and disadvantages of using both research approaches in answering your research question. Describe in detail how you could incorporate both research approaches, quantitative and qualitative, in a single research study that answered the same research question. Present your results to the entire class.

5. *A Very Very Hard Question.* With the results of Question 4 in mind, and in groups of four, discuss in detail how you would incorporate an "applied research component" and a "pure research component" in your qualitative Study Cnd in your quantitative study. Present your results to the entire class.

LIBRARY EXERCISES

1. At your university library, find out where the professional social work journals are located. What is the easiest way to locate a particular social work journal? List the titles of three social work journals, their call numbers, and library locations.

2. Select a research article from one of the journals you listed for the above exercise. After reading the article, answer the following questions: (a) Was the goal of the study pure or applied? Explain in detail. (b) In your opinion, did the study's findings contribute to our knowledge base? Why, or why not? (c) Was the study quantitative and/or qualitative? Provide a rationale for your response. (d) Do you feel the article made some good points for you to use in your future employment as a social worker? Why, or why not.

NOTES ON CHAPTER 1

_____

_____

_____

_____

_____

_____

_____

_____

_____

_____

_____

_____

_____

_____

_____

_____

_____

_____

C h a p t e r   2

Science, Society, and Research

CHAPTER OUTLINE

SELF-STUDY EXERCISES

1. What is the general research problem area in Study C? In your opinion, does it have all of the four necessary criterion for a good research problem as outlined in the chapter? Discuss each criterion in reference to Study C in detail.

2. What factors do you believe may have motivated the selection of the general research problem in Study C? Would you have chosen to study the same research problem? Why or why not?

3. What is the specific research question in Study C? In your opinion, is it appropriately derived from the study's general research problem? Would you have formulated the same research question? Why or why not?

4. Do you believe the authors of Study C used a procedure similar to the one as outlined in the chapter to derive the research question from the research problem? Why or why not? What procedure would you have taken to derive the research question from the research problem? How would your procedure differ from the one used by the author of Study C? Discuss in detail.

5. Was the research problem in Study C exploratory, descriptive, or explanatory? Explain your answer in detail. How could the authors, investigating the same problem area, have conducted a similar study at the other two knowledge levels?

6. Was Study C an applied research study or a pure research study? Explain your response in detail.

7. Discuss the various factors that may have lead the author of Study C to become interested in the study's general problem area.

8. Take the general problem area of homelessness. Construct a potential research question using this general problem area at the exploratory level, at the descriptive level, and at the explanatory level. Make sure your research problems meet the criteria as outlined in the chapter.

9. Discuss the factors that are involved in selecting an "applied" research question verses the factors that are involved in selecting a "pure" research question. Discuss in detail. Discuss how one single research study answering one single research question can generate "applied" *and* "pure" knowledge. Provide a social work example.

10. List and discuss in detail the various forms of errors in reasoning. Provide a social work example in your discussion.

11. List and discuss the three main reasons why people are resistant to change. Provide a social work example in your discussion.

12. List and discuss the various motives for doing social work research. Provide a social work example in your discussion.

13. List and discuss the strengths and limitations of the research method. Provide an example of each on in relation to Study C.

14. List and discuss the three general types of validity. Provide a social work example for each one in your discussion. Relate these three concepts to Study C.

15. What is the main difference between sample generalizability and cross-population generalizability? Relate these concepts to Study C.

GROUP EXERCISES

1. In groups of four, choose a social work–related problem area. Derive an exploratory, a descriptive, and an explanatory research question from the general problem area. Present your problem areas to the class.

2. In groups of four, create a hypothetical *exploratory* research study that would require the participation of social work clients. Decide on the study's purpose (pure or applied) and the research methodology.

3. In groups of four, create a hypothetical *descriptive* research study that would require the participation of social work clients. Decide on the study's purpose (pure or applied) and the research methodology.

4. In groups of four, create a hypothetical *explanatory* research study that would require the participation of social work clients. Decide on the study's purpose (pure or applied) and the research methodology.

5. After hearing the responses to the above four group exercises, why do you think it is easier to do an exploratory study over a descriptive one, or a descriptive one over an explanatory one? Discuss in detail.

6. *A Very Hard Question.* At this very beginning point in your social work research course, and after reading Box 1.5, in groups of four, discuss the various cultural factors that you feel need to be taken into account when formulating an *exploratory* research question. Do you feel any of these factors are different for formulating a qualitative research question verses a quantitative research question? an applied study verses a pure one? Discuss in detail and provide one common social work example in your Discussion. Report back to the entire class what your group found. Repeat this group exercise using *descriptive* research questions and *explanatory* research questions.

7. *A Very Very Hard Question.* At this very beginning point in your social work course, and in groups of four, design one single *qualitative* research study that proposes to answer three types of social work–related research questions of your choice, exploratory, descriptive, and explanatory. With the same research questions, design a *quantitative* research study. Compare the advantages and disadvantages of using both research approaches when it comes to formulating specific research questions from general problem areas.

LIBRARY EXERCISE

1. At your university library, locate a research article on a social work–related topic of your choice. Answer the following six questions in detail: (a) What is the general problem area? (b) What is the specific research question? (b) Was the study exploratory, descriptive, explanatory, or evaluative? (c) Was the study pure or applied? (d) What do you feel were the strengths and limitations of the study?

This chapter utilizes Study C

C h a p t e r 3

Research Contexts

CHAPTER OUTLINE

SELF-STUDY EXERCISES

1. List and discuss in detail the factors that affect social work research studies. Provide a social work example throughout your entire discussion.

2. Discuss how the factors mentioned above are highly interrelated with one another. After reading Study C, discuss how each one of

these factors my have affected the research study in its own individual way.

GROUP EXERCISE

1. *A Hard Question.* At this very beginning point in your social work research course, and after rereading Box 1.5, and in groups of four, discuss the various cultural factors that you feel need to be taken into account when considering each factor that affects social work research studies. Do you feel any of these factors are different for doing a qualitative study verses a quantitative one; an applied study verses a pure one? Discuss in detail and provide one common social work example in your discussion. Report back to the entire class what your group found.

NOTES ON CHAPTER 3

_____

_____

_____

_____

_____

_____

_____

_____

_____

_____

_____

_____

_____

_____

This chapter utilizes Study D

C h a p t e r   4

Research Ethics

CHAPTER OUTLINE

SELF-STUDY EXERCISES

1 Explain why social work research studies, such as Study D must follow strict ethical guidelines. Would you have done anything

differently to ensure that Study D was more ethically carried out? Why or why not?

2. In your opinion, how did the authors of Study D safeguard against possible concerns with violation of client rights? Discuss in detail.

3. Why was it necessary that the clients who participated in Study D participated on a voluntary basis? What, in your opinion, would have been the consequences of nonvoluntary participation? Justify your answer.

4. In your opinion, were the clients used in Study D competent to provide informed consent? Justify your answer.

5. In your opinion, how much and what kind of information would you consider adequate for obtaining a client's consent in Study D? What do you believe were the most important points to explain to these clients before embarking on the study? Justify your answer.

6. What were, in your opinion, the possibilities for coercing or rewarding the clients in Study D to participate? Discuss in detail.

7. Do you believe that the research approach used in Study D could harm the clients in any way? Justify your answer.

8. Do you believe that there was an appropriate balance between the provision of information and the disclosure of the study's purpose as outlined in Study D? Discuss in detail. How could the participants' knowledge of the study's purpose have influenced the outcome in Study D? Discuss in detail.

9. Do you believe that the issues of confidentiality in Study D were considered in the disclosure of the study's results? Why or why not?

GROUP EXERCISES

1. In groups of four, discuss the importance of ethics in social work. How do ethical considerations affect social work research? Discuss the dangers of conducting research in an unethical manner. As a class, discuss the ethical guidelines for research as outlined in the chapter and any problems that might arise from adhering to or ignoring these guidelines.

2. In groups of four, create a hypothetical research study that would require the participation of social work clients. Decide on the study's purpose and the research methodology. Discuss how you would protect the participants from harm, ensure confidentiality, provide

adequate information about the study, and encourage voluntary participation. Draft an informed consent statement that would address your ethical concerns. Read the statement to the class.

3. *A Hard Question*. At this very beginning point in your social work research course, and after rereading Boxes 1.5 and 4.1, in groups of four, discuss the various cultural factors that you feel need to be taken into account when writing a consent form. Do you feel any of these factors are different for doing a qualitative study verses a quantitative one; an applied study verses a pure one? Discuss in detail and provide one common social work example in your discussion. Report back to the entire class what your group found.

4. *A Very Hard Question*. At this very beginning point in your social work course, and in groups of four, design a qualitative research study that proposes to answer a social work–related research question of your choice. With the same research question, design a quantitative research study. Compare the advantages and disadvantages of using both research approaches when it comes to gaining the permission for someone to become a research participant. Present your results to the entire class.

5. *A Very Very Hard Question*. In groups of four, discuss in detail how you would go about gaining a client's permission to participate in an "applied" research study and in a "pure" research study. What are the main differences between getting a client to participate in a "pure" study verses an "applied" study? After rereading Box 1.5, discuss any cultural differences that need to be taken into account when gaining a client's consent to participate in a "pure" research study and in an "applied" one. Present your results to the entire class.

LIBRARY EXERCISES

1. At your university library, search the key words of *ethics* and *social work* on any computerized information retrieval system. Prepare a brief statement of the number and types of references you located.

2. At your university library, locate a social work–related research article. Discuss the author's research methodology in terms of its compliance with the ethical guidelines as outlined in the chapter. On the basis of your readings, answer the following five questions: (a) How were the possible sources of physical and mental harm to the participants minimized? (b) What information was provided to the

participants to ensure their informed and voluntary consent? (c) How was the competence of the participants ensured? (d) How was the confidentiality of information ensured? (e) What were the ethical strengths and weaknesses of the study's methodology? Discuss each one in detail.

NOTES ON CHAPTER 4

_____

_____

_____

_____

_____

_____

_____

_____

_____

_____

_____

_____

_____

_____

_____

_____

_____

_____

_____

_____

_____

C h a p t e r 5

Formulating Research Questions

CHAPTER OUTLINE

SELF-STUDY EXERCISES

1. What is the general research problem area in Study D? In your opinion, does it have all of the necessary characteristics of useful questions as contained in the chapter? Discuss each criterion in reference to Study D in detail.

2. What factors do you believe may have motivated the selection of the general research problem in Study D? Would you have chosen to study the same research problem (see Chapter 3)? Why or why not?

3. What is the specific research question in Study D? In your opinion, is it appropriately derived from the study's general research problem? Would you have formulated the same research question? Why or why not?

4. Do you believe the authors of Study D used a procedure similar to the one as outlined in the chapter to derive the research question from the research problem? Why or why not? What procedure would you have taken to derive the research question from the research problem? How would your procedure differ from the one used by the author of Study D? Discuss in detail.

5. Was the research problem in Study D exploratory, descriptive, or explanatory (see Chapter 2)? Explain your answer in detail. How could the author, investigating the same problem area, have conducted a similar study at the other two knowledge levels given the various characteristics of useful questions as outlined in this chapter?

6. Take the general problem area of homelessness. Construct a potential research question using this general problem area at the exploratory level, at the descriptive level, at the explanatory level, and at the evaluative level (Chapter 2), and address each one of the characteristics of useful research questions as contained in this chapter.

7. List and discuss the various sociocultural origins of research questions. Provide one example in your discussion

8. What are the main differences between researchable and nonresearchable questions? Provide and example of each one.

GROUP EXERCISES

1. In groups of four, choose a social work–related problem area. Derive an exploratory, a descriptive, an explanatory, and an evaluative research question from the general problem area (Chapter 2). Does each research problem have the necessary characteristics for useful research questions as presented in this chapter? Why or why not? Discuss the differences and the similarities among these criteria in relation to the four research questions. Present your findings to the class.

LIBRARY EXERCISE

1. At your university library, locate a research article on a social work–related topic of your choice. Answer the following six questions in detail: (a) What is the general problem area? (b) What is the specific research question? (c) Was the study exploratory, descriptive, or explanatory? (d) Was the study carried out in an ethical manner? (e) Did the study have relevancy, researchability, feasibility, and ethical acceptability? (f) Was the study pure or applied?

NOTES ON CHAPTER 5

_____

_____

_____

_____

_____

_____

_____

_____

_____

_____

C h a p t e r   6

Research Approaches

CHAPTER OUTLINE

SELF-STUDY EXERCISES

1. In your own words, discuss what is meant by the quantitative research approach to knowledge generation. In your opinion, what might the implications have been for the results in Study A if a quantitative research approach had *not* used?

2. What are the limitations of defining *quantitative* by the hypothetico-deductive method? Do you believe that Study A possessed any of these limitations? Explain in detail.

3. Discuss the characteristics of quantitative research studies as opposed to the characteristics of obtaining knowledge via tradition, authority, intuition, and practice wisdom methods as outlined in Chapter 1.

4. Discuss the process of selecting problem areas and formulating research questions within quantitative studies.

5. Discuss all of the steps of doing a quantitative research study. Use an example throughout your entire response.

6. What are the concepts and variables contained in Study A?

7. In what other manner could the variables have been conceptualized and operationalized in Study A? Discuss in detail.

8. Discuss the sequencing of steps in the quantitative research process. List, in your opinion, the sequence of steps that were utilized in Study A. Do you believe that the flexibility of the steps played an important role in carrying out Study A? Discuss in detail.

9. Discuss the ethical considerations associated with quantitative research studies such as Study A (Chapter 4). What were, in your opinion, the ethical limitations associated with the authors' choice of the quantitative research approach? Justify your answer.

10. Discuss the advantages and disadvantages of the quantitative research approach to knowledge generation. Use one common example throughout your discussion.

11. In your opinion, was the qualitative research approach the appropriate one to use in Study F? Why or why not?

12. What types of qualitative research questions are addressed in Study F? Discuss in detail.

13. How are the steps of the qualitative research process as outlined in the chapter different from those as presented in Study F? Discuss your answer in detail.

14. How, in your opinion, would the data collection methods used in Study F change if a quantitative research approach had been used?

15. What type of interview(s) was used in Study F? What type of interview would you have used? Why?

16. Do you believe that the use of focus groups would have been of benefit in Study F? Justify your answer.

17. Do you believe that a quantitative research approach could have been used in Study F? Justify your answer. How would the findings from a qualitative study differ from those of a quantitative study? Discuss in detail and relate your answer to Study F.

18. What ethical considerations do you believe guided the author of Study F? Discuss in detail.

19. In your own words, discuss what is meant by the qualitative research approach to knowledge generation. In your opinion, what might the implications have been for the results in Study F if a qualitative research approach had *not* used?

20. Discuss the process of selecting problem areas and formulating research questions within qualitative research studies. Compare and contrast your response to quantitative research studies.

21. Discuss all of the steps in doing a qualitative research study. Use a social work example throughout your entire response.

22. What are the concepts and variables contained in Study F? How would have they been conceptualized differently if a quantitative study had taken place?

23. In what other manner could the variables have been conceptualized and operationalized in Study F? Discuss in detail.

24. Discuss the sequencing of steps in the qualitative research process. List, in your opinion, the sequence of steps that were utilized in Study F. Do you believe that the flexibility of the steps played an important role in carrying out Study? Discuss in detail.

25. Discuss the ethical considerations associated with qualitative research studies such as Study F. What were, in your opinion, the ethical limitations associated with the author's choice of the qualitative research approach? Justify your answer.

26. Discuss the advantages and disadvantages of the qualitative research approach to knowledge generation. Use one common example throughout your discussion.

GROUP EXERCISES

1. *A Hard Question*. At this very beginning point in your social work research course, and after rereading Box 1.5, and in groups of four, discuss the various cultural factors that you feel need to be taken into account when doing a quantitative social work research study. Do you feel any of these factors are different for doing an "applied" study verses a "pure" one? Discuss in detail and provide one common social work example in your discussion. Report back to the entire class what your group found.

2. *A Very Hard Question*. At this very beginning point in your social work research course, and in groups of four, design a quantitative research study that proposes to answer a social work–related research question of your choice. Describe in detail how you could incorporate both an "applied" research component and a "pure" research component in the same quantitative study. Present your results to the entire class.

3. *A Very Hard Question*. At this very beginning point in your social work research course, and in groups of four, design a quantitative research study that proposes to answer a social work–related research question of your choice. With the same research question, design a qualitative research study. Compare the advantages and disadvantages of using both research approaches in answering your research question. Describe in detail how you could incorporate both research approaches, quantitative and qualitative, in a single research study that answered the same research question. Present your results to the entire class.

4. *A Very Very Hard Question*. With the results of Question 3 in mind, and in groups of four, discuss in detail how you would incorporate an "applied research component" and a "pure research component" in your qualitative study and in your quantitative study. Present your results to the entire class.

LIBRARY EXERCISES

1. At your university library, locate a social work–related journal article that used a quantitative research approach. Using what you know about quantitative research, answer the following nine questions: (a) What was the problem area and research question? What were the study's concepts, independent variables, dependent variables, and operational definitions? (b) What were the hypotheses (if any)? (c) What were the extraneous variables (if any)? (d) Evaluate the study's research hypothesis in relation to the criteria as outlined in the chapter. (e) Was the hypothesis one- or two-tailed? (f) What were some rival hypotheses that the study could have contained? (g) How did the author overcome the primary limitations of doing a quantitative study? (h) Did the author question any collective subjective beliefs? If so, what were they? (i) Did the quantitative study incorporate "human concern" for the client with effective social work practice? Explain, providing examples from the study.

2. At your university library, locate a social work–related journal article (four articles in total) where its main objective was to:
    - Describe variables and relationships
    - Predict and compare outcomes
    - Analyze components of interventions
    - Determine causal analyses

    Knowing what you know about quantitative research at this point, comment on how each article met its objective.

3. Using one of the four journal articles above, comment on how well it strived toward:
    - Measurability
    - Objectivity
    - Reducing uncertainty
    - Duplication
    - Using standardized procedures

4. Using one of the four journal articles above, comment on how well its author(s):
    - Selected a problem area
    - Conceptualized variables
    - Operationalized variables
    - Identified constants and labeled variables

- Formulated a research hypothesis
- Developed a sampling plan
- Selected a data collection method
- Analyzed the data

5. At your university library, locate a social work–related journal article that used a qualitative research approach. Using what you know about qualitative research, answer the following five questions: (a) What was the problem area and research question? (b) What were the study's concepts, independent variables, dependent variables, and operational definitions? (c) How did the author overcome the limitations of doing a qualitative study? (d) Did the author question any collective subjective beliefs? If so, what were they? (e) Did the qualitative study incorporate "human concern" for the client with effective social work practice? Explain, providing examples from the study.

6. Using the above journal article, comment on how well its author(s):
   - Selected a problem area
   - Selected research participants
   - Selected a site or setting
   - Gained permission and access to the field
   - Entered the field and identified key informants
   - Selected a research design and data collection method
   - Recorded, logged, and analyzed the data

NOTES ON CHAPTER 6

_____

_____

_____

_____

_____

_____

_____

_____

C h a p t e r 7

Utilization of Research Approaches

CHAPTER OUTLINE

SELF-STUDY EXERCISES

1. Discuss the epistemological origins of the quantitative and qualitative research approaches.

2. List and discuss the patterns of how the quantitative and qualitative research approaches have been utilized in social work research.

3. Discuss the myths that surround both research approaches to the generation of knowledge in our profession. Use a separate social work example for each myth.

4. Discuss how the quantitative and qualitative research approaches can both be used to generate useful knowledge for the social work profession. Provide a social work example throughout your discussion.

GROUP EXERCISES

1. Read Study C. In groups of four, discuss how the authors could have utilized a qualitative approach to study the same problem area. Be specific in your response. Present your results to the entire class for their opinion.

2. Read Study F. In groups of four, discuss how the author could have utilized a quantitative approach to study the same problem area. Be specific in your response. Present your results to the entire class for their opinion.

NOTES ON CHAPTER 7

_____

_____

_____

C h a p t e r 8

Measuring Variables

CHAPTER OUTLINE

SELF-STUDY EXERCISES

1. Discuss why measurement is fundamental to social work research. Discuss the common components of the definitions of measurement as outlined in the chapter. Discuss how the measurement process is different from, and similar to, the quantitative and qualitative research approaches.

2. List and discuss the functions of measurement in the social work research process as outlined in the chapter. Discuss how measurement functions are different from, and similar to, the quantitative and qualitative research approaches.

3. Discuss what is meant by measurement validity. Provide an example of measurement validity via a social work example. Discuss how measurement validity is different from, and similar to, the quantitative and qualitative research approaches.

4. Discuss what is meant by measurement reliability. Provide an example of measurement reliability via a social work example. Discuss how measurement reliability is different from, and similar to, the quantitative and qualitative research approaches.

5. Discuss the relationship between measurement validity and measurement reliability as presented in this chapter. Provide a quantitative and qualitative social work example throughout your discussion.

6. List and discuss the potential sources of measurement error as outlined in the chapter. Discuss how these errors are different from, and similar to, the quantitative and qualitative research approaches.

7. Discuss how a measuring instrument is assessed for its content validity. How can you tell if an instrument is content valid? Discuss how content validity is different from, and similar to, the quantitative and qualitative research approaches.

8. What is face validity? What is the difference between content validity and face validity? Provide a social work example throughout your discussion.

9. What is the difference between concurrent validity and predictive validity? Describe a situation in which you would use an instrument that has concurrent validity. Describe a situation in which you would use an instrument that has predictive validity. Discuss how concurrent validity and predictive validity are different from, and similar to, the quantitative and qualitative research approaches.

10. What does the test-retest method of reliability determine? Provide a social work example of how it could be used.

11. What is the alternate-forms method of reliability? Discuss how it could be determined in a social work situation.

12. What is the split-half method of reliability? Discuss how it could be determined in a social work situation.

13. Discuss the various cultural factors that you feel need to be taken into account (see Box 1.5) when it comes to the measurement process in social work research.

GROUP EXERCISES

1. In groups of four, construct a 10-item self-administered questionnaire that measures a variable of your choice. What difficulties, if any, did you have with the construction of the questionnaire? As a class, discuss each questionnaire and the problems associated with its construction.

2. Choose one of the questionnaires developed in the above exercise and have the entire class fill it out. What were some of the problems encountered? Was the questionnaire understandable and answerable? Using Figure 8.1, explain if the questionnaire was both valid and reliable. What methods would you use to improve the validity and the reliability of this self-administered questionnaire?

3. In groups of four, discuss how the process of measurement is different in a quantitative study when compared to a qualitative one. Present your results to the entire class.

4. *A Very Very Hard Question*. After reading the first seven chapters and Box 1.5 in this book, in groups of four, discuss the various cultural factors that you feel need to be taken into account when delineating and measuring variables in a *qualitative* social work research study. Do you feel any of these factors are different for doing an "applied" *qualitative* study verses a "pure" one? Discuss in detail. Report back to the entire class what your group found.

5. *A Very Very Hard Question*. After reading the first seven chapters and Box 1.5, in groups of four, discuss the various cultural factors that you feel need to be taken into account when delineating and measuring variables in a *quantitative* social work research study. Do you feel any of these factors are different for doing an "applied" *quantitative* study verses a "pure" one? Discuss in detail. Report back to the entire class what your group found.

LIBRARY EXERCISE

1. At your university library, locate a social work–related article that makes use of a measuring instrument. If the measuring instrument is not included in the article, find a copy of the instrument. Using what you know about measuring instruments answer the following two questions: (a) How were the validity and reliability of the instrument demonstrated? (b) Were any measurement errors mentioned? How were these errors compensated for or corrected?

NOTES ON CHAPTER 8

_____

_____

_____

_____

_____

_____

_____

_____

_____

_____

C h a p t e r 9

Measuring Instruments

CHAPTER OUTLINE

SELF-STUDY EXERCISES

1. Discuss the role that standardized measuring instruments plays in the social work research process. Provide a social work example throughout your discussion.

2. List and discuss in detail the six questions that must be asked when selecting a standardized measuring instrument. Provide a simple social work example throughout your discussion.

3. List and discuss in detail the advantages of using standardized measuring instruments. Provide a social work example throughout your discussion.

4. List and describe the various formats that standardized measuring instruments can take. Provide a social work example of each format.

5. What are the differences between rating scales and questionnaire-type scales? Discuss the advantages and disadvantages of each. Provide a social work example throughout your discussion.

6. List and discuss the four different kinds of rating scales. Discuss the advantages and disadvantages of each. Provide a social work example throughout your discussion.

7. List and discuss the two different kinds of modified scales. Discuss the advantages and disadvantages of each. Provide a social work example throughout your discussion.

8. What are nonstandardized measuring instruments? Compare these instruments with standardized ones. Provide a social work example throughout your discussion.

9. List and discuss in detail the advantages and disadvantages of using nonstandardized measuring instruments. Provide a social work example throughout your discussion.

10. Do you feel the *ISE* as presented in Figure 9.1 has all the criteria to be classified as a standardized measuring instrument? Explain your answer in detail.

11. Discuss the two methods of maximizing the content validity of measuring instruments.

12. Using the points in the chapter, discuss how the response categories, continuum of ratings, and length of a measuring instrument can be determined.

13. Discuss the concepts of external and internal validity as they relate to the construction of standardized measuring instruments. Discuss in detail.

14. Using the points as outlined in the chapter, compare and contrast rating scales with questionnaire-type scales.

GROUP EXERCISES

1. In groups of four, construct a brief 10-item questionnaire that measures a social work–related variable of your choice. What difficulties, if any, did you have with the selection of the response categories and the continuum of ratings? Discuss each questionnaire and the problems in its construction with the entire class.

2. Choose one of the questionnaires developed in the above exercise and have the entire class fill it out. What were some of the problems encountered? Was the questionnaire understandable and answerable? Explain if the questionnaire was both valid and reliable. What methods would you use to improve the validity and the reliability of this self-administered questionnaire?

3. In groups of four, compare and contrast the advantages and the disadvantages of rating scales versus questionnaire-type scales as used in social work research. Construct a 10-item questionnaire on a social work–related topic of your choice. In developing the questions, use each of the rating and questionnaire-type scales discussed in this chapter. Label each question with the type of scale used. Present your questionnaire to the class.

4. In groups of four, discuss how the process of measurement is different in a quantitative research study when compared to a qualitative research study. Present your results to the entire class.

LIBRARY EXERCISE

1. At your university library, locate a standardized measurement instrument related to social work. Answer the following four questions: (a) How do you believe the measurement need was determined? Discuss in detail. (b) What type(s) of scale(s) is(are) utilized in the instrument? (c) How does the author demonstrate the instrument's internal and external validity? (d) Evaluate the instrument. What are its advantages and disadvantages?

NOTES ON CHAPTER 9

_____

_____

_____

_____

_____

_____

_____

_____

_____

_____

_____

_____

_____

_____

> This chapter utilizes Study K

C h a p t e r   10

Designing Measuring Instruments

CHAPTER OUTLINE

SELF-STUDY EXERCISES

1. Using the points as outlined in the chapter, list and briefly discuss the six functions of measuring instruments.

2. Explain the functions of the measuring instrument contained in Figure 10.3. Support your answer by applying each of the six functions to the instrument.

3. Do you believe Figure 10.3 is externally valid? Why or why not? Using the points as outlined in the chapter, explain what steps were (or should have been) taken to ensure the instrument's external validity.

4. Do you believe Figure 10.3 is internally valid? Why or why not? Using the instrument design procedures as outlined in the chapter, discuss the aspects which contributed to and/or diminished the instrument's internal validity.

5. Using the points as outlined in the chapter, compare and contrast open-ended and closed-ended questions. What are the advantages and the disadvantages of using such questions? Discuss in detail.

6. Using Figure 10.3 as an example, discuss the eight factors to consider when designing a measuring instrument. Do you believe the author of the measuring instrument contained in Figure 10.3 considered any of the above factors when constructing it? Why or why not? Which factors do you believe were most important to consider? Why?

7. What is the purpose of pretesting a measuring instrument? Why do you believe it was necessary to pretest standardized measuring instruments?

8. What was the measuring instrument used in Study K? This is a trick question so be careful.

GROUP EXERCISES

1. In groups of four, construct a 10-item questionnaire. Did the group agree on the wording of the questions? Their meaning? How would you go about ensuring external and internal validity of the questions? How would you pretest your questionnaire? Present your questionnaire for discussion to the class.

2. In the same groups as for the above exercise, exchange your group's questionnaire with that of another group. Independently complete the questionnaire. Did all of the members in your group interpret the questions in the same manner? What questions were the focus of disagreement? What problems can your group predict in using the questionnaire to gather data? What are some possible solutions to these problems? Formulate a short list of do's and don't's for questionnaire construction. Discuss your list with the class.

LIBRARY EXERCISES

1. At your university library, locate a social work–related research article that describes the development of a standardized measurement instrument. Using the points as outlined in the chapter, answer the following five questions: (a) What function(s) does the instrument serve? (b) What steps were taken to ensure the instrument's external validity? Would you use the same steps? Why or why not? (c) What steps were taken to ensure the instrument's internal validity? Would you use the same steps? Why or why not? (d) Are the questions in the instrument open-ended, closed-ended, or a combination of the two types? What do you believe was the purpose of choosing the particular type(s) or question(s) used? Explain in detail. (e) Do you believe that the author pretested the questionnaire? Why or why not? How would you have gone about pretesting the questionnaire?

2. At your university library, locate two articles that discuss the construction of social work–related measuring instruments. How do the points as outlined in the chapter differ from those in the two articles? Do you believe any other guidelines may be necessary in instrument construction? If so, what are they?

NOTES ON CHAPTER 10

C h a p t e r   11

Sampling

CHAPTER OUTLINE

SELF-STUDY EXERCISES

1. Discuss how sampling theory assists in the process of social work research. Why, in your opinion, were the sampling methods used in Study B? Explain in detail.

2. Discuss the purpose and the use of sampling frames in social work research. Describe the sampling frame in Study B. Was the sampling frame in Study B identical to the study's population? Why or why not?

3. Discuss the issue of generalizability in social work research. Do you believe the sample used in Study B was representative of the population from which it was drawn? Why or why not?

4. Discuss the differences between probability and nonprobability sampling. What are their comparative advantages and disadvantages? Justify your answer by using the points as outlined in the chapter.

5. List and discuss the different types of probability sampling procedures. Do you believe any probability sampling procedures were used in Study B? Why or why not? In your explanation discuss the sampling techniques used in Study B as outlined in the chapter.

6. Discuss the procedure of generating a random sample. Explain how the author of Study B might have used Table 11.1 to generate a random sample. Discuss the process in detail.

7. List and briefly discuss the different types of nonprobability sampling procedures.

8. Discuss how sampling errors vary with the size of the sample.

9. What, in your opinion, was the potential for sampling error in Study B? Discuss in detail.

10. List and discuss the various forms of nonsampling errors. What, in your opinion, may have been some of the nonsampling errors that may have occurred in Study B?

11. What suggestions could you provide to minimize nonsampling errors?

GROUP EXERCISES

1. Suppose you wanted the students in your class to participate in a research study. In groups of four, discuss what random sampling procedures could be used. Using Table 11.1, decide on a procedure,

discuss how you would collect the data, and explain your decisions to the class. How does your study compare with those of the other groups? Discuss the problems associated with random sampling and possible solutions to the problems.

2. Suppose you design a research project that concerns all of the students of your university. In groups of four, decide on a sample size and discuss how you could use the four nonprobability sampling methods. Discuss the potential problems and possible solutions to the problems.

LIBRARY EXERCISES

1. At your university library, locate a social work–related research study that used a *probability* sampling procedure. Answer the following five questions: (a) What sampling procedure was used? (b) From what general population was the sample drawn? (c) Do you believe that the sample was representative of the population from which it was drawn? Why or why not? (d) What other sampling procedure could have been used? What would be the implications if this sampling method were used? (e) What changes could you suggest that would make the study more rigorous in terms of sampling procedures and/or controlling for nonsampling errors? Discuss in detail.

2. At your university library, locate a social work–related research study that used a *nonprobability* sampling procedure. Answer the following three questions: (a) What sampling procedure was used? (b) Could the author have used a different nonprobability sampling procedure? If so, which one? (c) In your opinion, does probability sampling or do nonprobability sampling procedures produce a more rigorous study? Justify your answer.

NOTES ON CHAPTER 11

_____

_____

_____

_____

C h a p t e r   12

Group Research Designs

CHAPTER OUTLINE

SELF-STUDY EXERCISES

1. Discuss why very few social work research studies ever come close to "ideal" experiments. What are some of the reasons why it would be unethical to do "ideal" experiments with clients?

2. Discuss in detail each one of the six characteristics that are necessary to approach an "ideal" experiment in social work research. Provide a social work example in your discussion.

3. Design an "ideal" experiment with the general problem area of child sexual abuse.

4. Construct an "ideal" explanatory-level experiment with the research problem of suicide. What ethical problems did you run into?

5. Construct an "ideal" explanatory-level experiment with the research problem of abortion. What ethical problems did you run into?

6. In your own words, discuss why it is important for you to know the six characteristics of an "ideal" experiment when you design any given research study.

7. Why is it necessary to use at least one control group (or comparison group) when trying to design an "ideal" experiment?

8. Write an explanatory-level research hypothesis in which Variable A (some variable of your choice) is the independent variable and Variable B (some variable of your choice) is the dependent variable. Now rewrite the same hypothesis with the two variables reversed. Which hypothesis do you think is correct? Why? How would you go about testing the two hypotheses? Include in your discussion how you would address all six of the characteristics of an "ideal" experiment.

9. Discuss in detail the similarities and differences between the concepts of internal and external validity. Provide a social work example throughout your discussion.

10. List and discuss the threats to internal validity by using a common social work example of your choice.

11. List and discuss the threats to external validity by using a common social work example of your choice.

12. Design an "ideal" social work experiment that controls for all the threats to internal and external validity. You may select any topic that you desire.

13. List other factors that you feel could be added as additional threats to *internal validity* besides the ones presented in this chapter.

14. List other factors that you feel could be added as additional threats to *external validity* besides the ones presented in this chapter. Provide a rationale for your response.

15. Discuss the differences among trend studies, cohort studies, and panel studies. Use a social work example throughout your discussion.

16. List all the group research designs and indicate the threats to internal and external validity that each design controls for. Provide a rationale for each one of your responses. Provide a social work example to illustrate each one of your points.

17. Design a perfect group research study, at the explanatory level, that takes into account all the threats to internal and external validity. What ethical issues do you see if your study were in fact implemented?

18. Out of all the group research designs presented in this chapter, which one do you think is used most often in social work research? Why? Justify your answer. Which one do you think is least utilized? Why? Justify your answer.

GROUP EXERCISES

1. In groups of four, decide on a social work–related problem area. Design three hypothetical studies using one design from each of the three knowledge levels. For each study determine what data need to be gathered. Provide the graphic representation of the study detailing the Rs, Os, and Xs. Present the three designs to the entire class with a detailed explanation of the population and the sampling procedures.

2. In groups of four, discuss each of the threats to external validity and the threats to internal validity in the context of controlling for them. What problems do you foresee in attempting to control for all of the threats to internal and external validity? Present your discussion to the entire class.

LIBRARY EXERCISES

1. At your university library, identify a research article that comes

closest to an "ideal" experiment. What were the characteristics that were missing in the study that prevented it from becoming an "ideal" experiment?

2. With the article you selected for Question 1, hypothetically redesign the study using the six characteristics for an "ideal" experiment.

3. At your university library, identify two social work research articles that focused on the same topic area. Which study do you feel had the most *internal validity*. Why? Justify your response. Provide a rationale as to why it is necessary to have higher degrees of internal validity for research studies at descriptive or explanatory levels than at the exploratory level.

4. At your university library, choose two social work research articles that focused on the same topic area. Which study do you feel had the most *external validity*? Why? Justify your response. Provide a rationale as to why it is necessary to have higher degrees of external validity for research studies at the descriptive or explanatory levels than at the exploratory level.

5. At your university library, find a published social work research article that controlled for as many threats to internal and external validity as possible. Go through the article and determine which internal and external validity factors the study controlled for, and which factors it did not control for. Hypothetically redesign the study in such a way where you could control for the factors that the original study did not. After doing this, would your hypothetical redesigned study have been feasible? Discuss in detail.

6. At your university library, find a social work article that reports on a research study that used an *exploratory* research design. How could have this study been done using a "higher level" group research design?

7. At your university library, find a social work article that reports on a research study that used a *descriptive* research design. How could have this study been done using a "higher level" group research design?

NOTES ON CHAPTER 12

_____

_____

C h a p t e r   13

Case Research Designs

CHAPTER OUTLINE

SELF-STUDY EXERCISES

1. Discuss in detail how a case design "significantly" differs from a group design (Chapter 12).
2. Discuss the purpose of a "case" as used in a case study.
3. Discuss the issue of generalizability in case study research.
4. Discuss how similar and different sampling procedures can be used in reference to group designs and case study designs.
5. Discuss in detail how a case study design can be used in *client assessment*. Compare and contrast the advantages and disadvantages of using some group designs and case study designs to help social workers assess client situations.
6. Discuss in detail how a case study design can be used in *interventions*. Compare and contrast the advantages and disadvantages of using some group designs and case study designs to help social workers in the *interventive* process.
7. Discuss in detail how a case study design can be used in assessing *client outcomes*. Compare and contrast the advantages and disadvantages of using some group designs and case study designs to help social workers assess client outcomes.
8. Discuss the necessary criteria that need to be met to evaluate outcome-oriented case studies. Provide a social work example in your discussion.
9. How does a "case" represent itself? Discuss in detail.
10. Discuss the three skills that are needed when a social worker generalizes from one case to another.
11. Discuss the necessary criteria that need to be met for evaluating the conceptual framework for a case study.
12. Discuss the differences between deterministic and probabilistic causation. Provide a social work example of each in your discussion.
13. What are intervening and extraneous variables? Discuss how they are similar in case study research and in group research. Provide a social work example of each in your discussion.

14. Compare and contrast the necessary criteria that need to be met to evaluate the clarity and accuracy of findings generated from a case study research design and from a group research design.

GROUP EXERCISE

1. Have the entire class select one common social work–related problem area. In groups of four, discuss how the problem could be researched with a group research design (Chapter 12) *and* with a case study research design. What types of data would each design provide? What are the advantages of using a group design over a case study design, and vise versa? Discuss the generalizability of your hypothetical findings derived from your group design over your case study design. Have all groups report back to the entire class. What were the similarities and differences among the groups? Discuss the implications.

LIBRARY EXERCISES

1. At your university library, locate a social work–related research study (article) that used a group research design and another study (article) that used a case study design. Both studies must have addressed the same general problem area. What data did the study that used a group research design provide over the study that used a case study design, and vice versa? Discuss the advantages and disadvantages of using a case design over a group design with this problem area. Discuss how both types of designs, case and group, can be used to complement one another.

2. At your university library, locate an article that used a case study research design. Evaluate the article with the criteria presented in the chapter. How would you do the case study differently? Why? Discuss in detail using the contents of this chapter as a guide.

NOTES ON CHAPTER 13

Participant Observation

CHAPTER OUTLINE

SELF-STUDY EXERCISES

1. What is participant observation? List and discuss how it can be used in social work research studies. What are its advantages? What are its disadvantages? Provide a social work research situation where you would use this type of nonsurvey data collection method.

2. Using the points as outlined in the chapter, discuss the steps in using participant observation as a data collection method.

3. Discuss in detail how participant observation can be used as a data collection method in quantitative and research studies (Chapter 6). Provide one common social work example in your discussion.

4. Discuss in detail how participant observation can be used as a data collection method in group research studies (Chapter 12) and in case research studies (Chapter 13). Provide one common social work example in your discussion.

5. Using your own words, define participant observation. Discuss how can it be used as a "research method" and as a "data collection method." Provide a social work example in your discussion.

6. Discuss the distinguishing features of participant observation as outlined in the chapter. Provide a social work example in your discussion.

7. Discuss when it is appropriate to use participant observation as a data collection method. Provide a social work example in your discussion.

8. Discuss the minimal conditions that must be met to use participant observation as a data collection method. Provide a social work example in your discussion.

9. Discuss the continuum of participant observation roles. When should we use one over the other? Explain in detail. Provide a social work example in your discussion.

10. Discuss the four ways to gather data by the participant observation method of data collection. Provide a social work example in your discussion.

11. Discuss how survey research interviews (Chapter 15) are different from participant observation interviews. Provide a social work example in your discussion.

12. Discuss the three ways to record data when using participant observation as a data collection method. Provide a social work example in your discussion.

13. Discuss the four types of field notes. When do you use one over the other? Provide a social work example in your discussion.

14. Discuss the three approaches to recording data gathered in qualitative research interviews. Provide a social work example in your discussion.

15. Discuss the ethical issues involved in using participant observation as a data collection method. How are these ethical issues different than using structured observation or surveys as data collection methods? Discuss in detail.

GROUP EXERCISE

1. In groups of four, select one common social work–relevant topic area that you feel could be researched using participant observation as a data collection method. State a single research question and design two different research studies to answer your research question: one using a survey (Chapter 15) as a data collection method, and one using participant observation as a data collection method. What types of data would be generated from both data collection methods? Could you use both of them in a single study to answer the research question? Why, or why not? Explain in detail.

LIBRARY EXERCISES

1. At your university library, locate a social work–related research article that used participant observation as the data collection method. What potential problems did you feel the researcher(s) encountered in using this type of data collection methodology? What were the advantages of the data collection methodology used? Discuss your answers in detail.

2. For the study in Question 1, provide an in-depth critique using the contents of this chapter as a guide. Also, discuss areas of sampling, research design, operationalization of variables, generalizability, limitation, usefulness of findings, etc.

3. How would you have done the study in Question 1 differently, via a different data collection method, given the same research question? Discuss in detail and be very specific. Keep in mind the context of the study (Chapters contained in Part I in the book).

NOTES ON CHAPTER 14

_____

_____

_____

_____

_____

_____

_____

_____

_____

_____

_____

_____

_____

_____

_____

_____

_____

_____

C h a p t e r   15

Survey Research

CHAPTER OUTLINE

SELF-STUDY EXERCISES

1. Using the points as outlined in the chapter, discuss the steps in the survey research process. Discuss how the above steps are interrelated with one another. Discuss how the author of Study B would have had to follow the steps as outlined in Figure 15.1. Explain.

2. Discuss the use of survey research in exploratory, descriptive, and explanatory studies. In your opinion, at what level on the knowledge continuum is Study B? Justify your answer.

3. Compare and contrast the cross-sectional and longitudinal approaches to survey research. What approach(es) did the author of Study B use? Justify your answer with information highlighting the points as presented in the chapter.

4. Discuss the advantages and the disadvantages of face-to-face interviewing. Could the researcher in Study B have chosen the face-to-face interview as a method of data collection? Why or why not? What would be the advantages and disadvantages of using the face-to-face interview data collection method in Study B?

5. Discuss the differences between group-administered questionnaires and mail surveys. Explain in what situation each method would be most appropriate.

6. What does the acronym CATI stand for? Discuss the advantages and the disadvantages of CATI in relation to other forms of data collection. In your opinion, would CATI have been appropriate to use in Study B? Explain.

7. Discuss in detail how surveys can be used as a data collection method in quantitative research studies (Chapter 6) and in qualitative research studies (Chapter 6). Provide one common social work example in your discussion.

8. Discuss in detail how surveys can be used as a data collection method in group research studies (Chapter 12) and in case research studies (Chapter 13). Provide one common social work example in your discussion.

9. Describe in your own words the purpose of survey research. Why are surveys useful? Describe the steps that a survey research study would take in reference to finding out how satisfied social workers are with their social work education.

10. Describe in detail the two main data collection methods that can be used in survey research. Provide a social work example of each, using one common research problem. In other words, how could your survey be conducted using questionnaires or interviews? How could it have been conducted using both? Discuss the advantages and disadvantages of using the two primary data collection methods.

11. Discuss in detail the two types of questionnaires that can be used in survey research. In which situations is one better than the other? Provide a rationale for your response. Use a social work example to illustrate your points.

12. What are the two types of questions that can be included in a questionnaire or interview schedule? Provide a social work example of each.

13. When is an open-ended item better to use than a closed-ended item? Provide a rationale for your response.

14. Discuss the commonalities and differences between personal interviews and telephone interviews used in survey research. In which situation is one better than the other?

GROUP EXERCISES

1. In groups of six, develop a 10-item questionnaire to survey your classmates' opinions on an issue relevant to social work. Group-administer the questionnaire to your class. Collect the completed questionnaires and return to the same group of six. What problems occurred in using the group-administered questionnaire as a data collection method? What are some potential solutions to these problems? Formulate a list of do's and don't's for group-administered questionnaires. Present your list to the class.

2. In the same group of six, designate three people as interviewers and three people as interviewees. Conduct face-to-face interviews in pairs of two using the questionnaire developed in the exercise above. Return to your group and discuss the following four questions. (a) What problems occurred in using the interview to gather data? (b) How did your experiences compare with the problems discussed in

the chapter? (c) Which form of survey research would be best to use with your questionnaire? Why? (d) Would you revise your questionnaire? If so, how? Present your findings to the entire class.

LIBRARY EXERCISES

1. At your university library, locate a social work–related research article that used the survey as the data collection method. What type of survey research was used? What potential problems did you feel the researcher(s) encountered in using this type of data collection methodology? Discuss your answers in detail.

2. At your university library, locate a social work–related research article that used the mail survey method as the data collection method. What problems were encountered in collecting the data through the mail survey research method? What were the advantages of the data collection methodology used? Design a short hypothetical cover letter for the survey described in the article.

3. At your university library, locate a social work research article that used a mailed survey questionnaire to gather the data for the study. How could the study have used personal interviews rather than survey questionnaires to provide data to answer the research question? Provide a rationale for your response. What type of data would the interviews provide that the mailed questionnaire did not? Justify your answer.

4. For the study in Question 3, provide an in-depth critique using the contents of this chapter as a guide. Also, discuss areas of sampling, research design, operationalization of variables, generalizability, limitation, usefulness of findings, etc.

5. How would you have done the study in Question 3 differently, via a different survey method, given the same research question? Discuss in detail and be very specific. Keep in mind the context of the study (Chapter 2).

C h a p t e r   16

Secondary Analysis

CHAPTER OUTLINE

SELF-STUDY EXERCISES

1. Using the points as outlined in the chapter, define secondary analysis in your own terms. List some potential sources of data for a secondary analysis. Discuss in detail. What sources of data were used in Study C? Discuss in detail.

2. Compare and contrast the inductive and deductive processes in a secondary analysis. In your opinion, what process was used in Study C? Use the points as outlined in the chapter to support your answer.

3. Use the points as outlined in the chapter to discuss the use of secondary analysis in exploratory, descriptive, and explanatory research studies.

4. Discuss what is meant by reliability in a secondary analysis. Do you believe that the data used in Study C were reliable? Why or why not? Discuss in detail.

5. Discuss what is meant by validity in a secondary analysis. Do you believe that the data used in Study C were valid? Why or why not? Discuss in detail.

6. Using the points as outlined in the chapter, summarize the possible sources of error in a secondary analysis. Are any such errors present in Study C? Highlight each of the sources in your answer.

7. Discuss the problem of missing data in a secondary analysis. List the areas of missing data in Study C. Do you see any problems with data analyses when there are a lot of missing data? Explain. Do you believe that the missing data in Study C was influenced by any subjectivity or bias? Why or why not? Discuss in detail.

8. Discuss in detail the three types of data that are available for secondary analyses. Provide a social work example in your discussion.

9. Discuss in detail the specific steps of doing a secondary analysis using a social work problem area of your choice as an extended example.

10. List and discuss the four questions that need to be addressed when evaluating a data set. Provide a social work example in your discussion.

11. List and discuss in detail the advantages and disadvantages of doing a secondary analysis. As a data collection method, compare and contrast the advantages and disadvantages of secondary analyses with surveys (Chapter 15), and participant observation (Chapter 14).

12. Discuss in detail how secondary analyses can be used as a data collection method in quantitative research studies (Chapter 6) and in qualitative research studies (Chapter 6). Provide one common social work example in your discussion.

13. Discuss in detail how secondary analyses can be used as a data collection method in group research studies (Chapter 12) and in case research studies (Chapter 13). Provide one common social work example in your discussion.

GROUP EXERCISES

1. In groups of four, decide on a social work–related problem area. Describe how you could carry out a secondary analysis of this problem. In your description, define the research hypothesis, sample, and the sources of data. What instruments would you use to collect the data? What research design would be most appropriate? Present your discussion to the entire class.

2. In groups of four, and using the hypothetical study you created in the above exercise, answer the following three questions: (a) Did you use an inductive or deductive process? (b) What were the potential sources of error in your study? (c) How could you determine the reliability and validity of your data? Present your answers to the entire class.

LIBRARY EXERCISES

1. At your university library, locate a social work–related research article that used a secondary analysis as a data collection method. What problems do you believe were encountered in using this method? Construct a short 10-item measuring instrument that could have been completed by the author to supplement the existing data. How do you believe your measuring instrument would have improved the author's study?

2. Using the research article that you located for the above exercise, answer the following five questions: (a) Was an inductive or deductive process used? Justify your answer. (b) Was the study's design exploratory, descriptive, or explanatory? Explain. (c) Do you believe the data were reliable and valid? Why or why not? (d) What were the sources of error in the study? (e) What suggestions could you make to improve the study?

NOTES ON CHAPTER 16

_____

_____

_____

_____

_____

_____

_____

_____

_____

_____

_____

_____

_____

C h a p t e r   17

Utilizing Existing Statistics

CHAPTER OUTLINE

SELF-STUDY EXERCISES

1. In your own words and using the points as outlined in the chapter, define how you could use existing statistics as a data collection method.
2. List some potential sources of data for a utilizing existing statistics as a data collection method. Discuss in detail.
3. Discuss what is meant by reliability when utilizing existing statistics as a data collection method. Discuss in detail.
4. Discuss what is meant by validity when utilizing existing statistics as a data collection method. Discuss in detail.
5. Discuss in detail the specific steps that you would take if you did a research study that utilized existing statistics as a data collection method using a social work problem area of your choice as an extended example.
6. List and discuss in detail the advantages and disadvantages of doing a research study that utilized existing statistics as a data collection method. As a data collection method, compare and contrast the advantages and disadvantages of utilizing existing statistics with surveys (Chapter 15), participant observation (Chapter 14), and secondary analyses (Chapter 16).
7. Discuss in detail how utilizing existing statistics can be used as a data collection method in quantitative research studies (Chapter 6) and in qualitative research studies (Chapter 6). Provide one common social work example in your discussion.
8. Discuss in detail how utilizing existing statistics can be used as a data collection method in group research studies (Chapter 12) and in case research studies (Chapter 13). Provide one common social work example in your discussion.

GROUP EXERCISES

1. In groups of four, decide on a social work–related problem area. Describe how you could carry out a research study that utilized existing statistics as a data collection method. In your description, define the research hypothesis, sample, and the sources of data. What instruments would you use to collect the data? What research design would be most appropriate? Present your discussion to the

entire class.

2. In groups of four, and using the hypothetical study you created in the above exercise, answer the following three questions: (a) Did you use an inductive or deductive process? (b) What were the potential sources of error in your study? (c) How could you determine the reliability and validity of your data? Present your answers to the entire class.

LIBRARY EXERCISES

1. At your university library, locate a social work–related research article that utilized existing statistics as a data collection method. What problems do you believe were encountered in using this method? Construct a short 10-item measuring instrument that could have been completed by the author to supplement the existing data. How do you believe your measuring instrument would have improved the author's study?

2. Using the research article that you located for the above exercise, answer the following five questions: (a) Was an inductive or deductive process used? Justify your answer. (b) Was the study's design exploratory, descriptive, or explanatory? Explain. (c) Do you believe the data were reliable and valid? Why or why not? (d) What were the sources of error in the study? (e) What suggestions could you make to improve the study?

NOTES ON CHAPTER 17

_____

_____

_____

_____

_____

_____

_____

C h a p t e r   18

Content Analysis

CHAPTER OUTLINE

SELF-STUDY EXERCISES

1. Define content analysis. Discuss the similarities and differences between a secondary analysis and a content analysis.

2. Discuss the three characteristics of a content analysis as outlined in the chapter. How does each characteristic contribute to the validity and reliability in the research process? Does Study E demonstrate each of the three characteristics? Why or why not?

3. Discuss the four broad areas of classification in a content analysis as outlined in the chapter. How would you classify Study E? Justify your answer.

4. Discuss the process of developing the research question in studies that use content analysis as the method of data collection. In your opinion, what was the research question in Study E? Would you have formulated the same question? Why or why not?

5. Discuss the process of choosing the sample in studies that use content analysis as the method of data collection. Discuss the sampling methodology used in Study E. Would you have used the same sampling strategy? Why or why not?

6. Discuss the process of selecting the unit of analysis in studies that use content analysis as the method of data collection. What was the unit of analysis in Study E? What other unit of analysis could the authors of Study E have chosen?

7. Discuss the process of coding and analyzing data in studies that use content analyses as methods of data collection. Outline the procedure that was used in Study E for coding and analyzing the data. Would you have operationally defined the categories in the same way as the authors of Study E? Discuss in detail.

8. List and discuss in detail the advantages and disadvantages of doing a research study that utilized a content analysis as a data collection method. As a data collection method, compare and contrast the advantages and disadvantages of utilizing a content analysis with surveys (Chapter 15), participant observation (Chapter 14), secondary analyses (Chapter 16), and utilizing existing statistics (Chapter 17).

9. Discuss in detail how a content analysis can be used as a data collection method in quantitative research studies (Chapter 6) and in qualitative research studies (Chapter 6). Provide one common social work example in your discussion.

10. Discuss in detail how utilizing a content analysis can be used as a data collection method in group research studies (Chapter 12) and in case research studies (Chapter 13). Provide one common social work example in your discussion.

GROUP EXERCISES

1. In groups of four, decide on a social work–related problem area. Describe how you could carry out a research study that utilized a content analysis as a data collection method. In your description, define the research hypothesis, sample, and the sources of data. What instruments would you use to collect the data? What research design would be most appropriate? Present your discussion to the entire class.

2. In groups of four, and using the hypothetical study you created in the above exercise, answer the following three questions: (a) Did you use an inductive or deductive process? (b) What were the potential sources of error in your study? (c) How could you determine the reliability and validity of your data? Present your answers to the entire class.

LIBRARY EXERCISES

1. At your university library, locate a social work–related research article that utilized a content analysis as a data collection method. What problems do you believe were encountered in using this method? Construct a short 10-item measuring instrument that could have been completed by the author to supplement the existing data. How do you believe your measuring instrument would have improved the author's study?

2. Using the research article that you located for the above exercise, answer the following five questions: (a) Was an inductive or deductive process used? Justify your answer. (b) Was the study's design exploratory, descriptive, or explanatory? Explain. (c) Do you believe the data were reliable and valid? Why or why not? (d) What were the sources of error in the study? (e) What suggestions could you make to improve the study?

NOTES ON CHAPTER 18

_____

_____

_____

_____

_____

_____

_____

_____

_____

_____

_____

_____

_____

_____

_____

_____

_____

_____

_____

_____

_____

_____

_____

_____

_____

_____

_____

_____

_____

_____

_____

C h a p t e r   19

Selecting a Data Collection Method and Data Source

CHAPTER OUTLINE

SELF-STUDY EXERCISES

1. Discuss in detail what is meant by a data collection method. Provide a social work example in your discussion.

2. Discuss in detail what is meant by a data source. Provide a social work example in your discussion.

3. Discuss in detail how available data collection methods influence the selection of data sources, and vice versa. Provide a social work example in your discussion.

4. Discuss in detail how available data collection methods and data sources influence the selection of research problems and research questions, and vice versa. Provide a social work example in your discussion.

5. Discuss in detail how available data collection methods and data sources influence the selection of research designs, and vice versa. Provide a social work example in your discussion.

6. List and discuss in detail the criteria that can be used to select a data collection method. Provide a social work example in your discussion.

7. List and discuss in detail the criteria that can be used to select a data source. Provide a social work example in your discussion.

8. Describe in detail the main differences between obtrusive data collection methods and unobtrusive data collection methods. When would you chose one over the other? Discuss in detail. Provide a social work example in your discussion.

9. Describe in detail how you could use an unobtrusive data collection method along with an obtrusive one in a single research study that focused on one specific research question (or hypothesis). Provide a social work example in your discussion.

10. Describe in detail how you could use two or more different data sources in a single research study that focused on one specific research question (or hypothesis). Provide a social work example in your discussion.

11. Describe how Study E could have used a different data collection method and data source to answer the same research question. What other data would this new data collection method and data source generate that the original one (content analysis) did not?

12. Describe how Study F could have used a different data collection method and data source to answer the same research question. What other data would this new data collection method and data source generate that the original one (secondary analysis) did not?

GROUP EXERCISES

1. In groups of four, decide on a social work–related problem area. Derive a research question (or hypothesis) out of the problem area. Describe how you could carry out seven different hypothetical quantitative research studies that could answer your research question (or test your hypothesis) using each of the data collection methods listed on the top of Table 19.1. In your description, define all relevant variables (e.g., independent, dependent, extraneous, intervening), the research question (or hypothesis), potential rival hypotheses, the specific research design, the sample, the data collection method(s), and the data source(s) for each data collection method(s). Discuss the limitations of your hypothetical study. Present your discussion to the entire class.

2. Repeat Exercise 1 with seven different qualitative research studies.

3. Repeat Exercise 1 integrating a quantitative component and a qualitative component.

LIBRARY EXERCISES

1. At your university library, locate a social work–related research article that utilized any data collection method. What problems do you believe were encountered in using this method? What other method could the author have used to collect data? Why?

2. At your university library, locate a social work–related research article that utilized any data source. What problems do you believe were encountered in using this data source? What other data source could the author have used? Why? Discuss in detail.

3. Using the research article that you located for the above exercise, answer the following five questions: (a) Was an inductive or deductive process used? Justify your answer. (b) Was the study's design exploratory, descriptive, or explanatory? Explain. (c) Do you believe the data were reliable and valid? Why or why not? (d) What were the sources of error in the study? (e) What suggestions could you make to improve the study?

NOTES ON CHAPTER 19

_____

_____

_____

_____

_____

_____

_____

_____

_____

_____

_____

_____

_____

_____

_____

_____

_____

This chapter utilizes Studies A and F

C h a p t e r   20

Writing Research Proposals

CHAPTER OUTLINE

SELF-STUDY EXERCISES

1. Discuss in detail the three characteristics of research proposals. Provide a social work example in your discussion.
2. Discuss in detail the eleven components, or parts, of research proposals.
3. Write a research proposal, using the parts as headings, that you think could have been used for Study A.
4. Repeat Exercise 3 for Study F.
5. Discuss the similarities and difference between quantitative proposals (Study A) and qualitative proposals (Study F).

GROUP EXERCISES

1. In groups of four, decide on a social work–related problem area. Derive a quantitative research question (or hypothesis) out of the problem area and write a research proposal to do the study.
2. Repeat Exercise 1 for a qualitative study.

NOTES ON CHAPTER 20

_____

_____

_____

_____

_____

_____

_____

This chapter utilizes Study D	

C h a p t e r   21

Writing Research Reports

CHAPTER OUTLINE

SELF-STUDY EXERCISES

1. Discuss in detail the organization and content of research reports. Provide examples of how Study D was organized, or was not organized, around these concepts.
2. Discuss in detail how to submit a research report for possible publication.
3. Write a hypothetical research report using the results from a hypothetical quantitative study.
4. Repeat Exercise 3 for a qualitative study.

NOTES ON CHAPTER 21

_____

_____

_____

_____

_____

_____

_____

_____

_____

_____

_____

_____

_____

_____

_____

_____

_____

C h a p t e r   22

Evaluating Research Reports

CHAPTER OUTLINE

SELF-STUDY EXERCISES

1. Discuss in detail each one of the four general criterion for evaluating research reports. Discuss the importance of each criterion to social work practice. Provide a social work example in your discussion.

2. Using the five figures in Chapter 22, evaluate Study B. What did your evaluation tell you? Was Study B useful to you as a social worker? Why, or why not?

NOTES ON CHAPTER 22

_____

_____

_____

_____

_____

_____

_____

_____

_____

_____

_____

_____

_____

C h a p t e r   23

Single-System Designs

CHAPTER OUTLINE

SELF-STUDY EXERCISES

1. Discuss in your own words the purpose of case-level evaluation designs (Single-subject designs). Use a social work example throughout your discussion.

2. List and discuss in detail the three requirements that case-level evaluation designs must have in order for them to be useful to social work practitioners and researchers. Use a social work example throughout your discussion.

3. List and discuss in detail the three *exploratory* case-level evaluation designs. Provide a social work example of each.

4. List and discuss in detail the two *descriptive* case-level evaluation designs. Provide a social work example of each.

5. List and discuss in detail the three *explanatory* case-level evaluation designs. Provide a social work example of each.

6. What do descriptive case-level evaluation designs have that exploratory ones do not? Provide a social work example in your discussion.

7. What do explanatory case-level evaluation designs have that descriptive ones do not? Provide a social work example in your discussion.

8. What is the major purpose of multiple-baseline case-level evaluation designs? Discuss in detail. Provide a social work example of all three types.

9. List and discuss in detail the advantages and disadvantages of case-level evaluation designs. Provide a social work example throughout your discussion.

10. When is it inappropriate to implement an *A*-phase when trying to achieve a case-level research design? Provide a social work example throughout your discussion.

11. In your own words, discuss the similarities and differences between case-level evaluation designs and group research designs as presented in Chapter 12. Use a social work example throughout your discussion.

12. In your own words, discuss the similarities and differences between *exploratory* case-level evaluation designs and *exploratory* group research designs as presented in Chapter 12. Use a social work example throughout your discussion.

13. In your own words, discuss the similarities and differences between *descriptive* case-level evaluation designs and *descriptive* group research designs as presented in Chapter 12. Use a social work example throughout your discussion.

14. In your own words, discuss the similarities and differences between *explanatory* case-level evaluation designs and *explanatory* group research designs as presented in Chapter 12. Use a social work example throughout your discussion.

15. Design a perfect explanatory case-level evaluation study that takes into account all the threats to internal and external validity mentioned in Chapter 12. What ethical issues do you see if your study was in fact implemented?

16. Out of all the case-level evaluation designs presented in this chapter, which one do you think is used most often in social work research? Why? Justify your answer. Which one do you think is least utilized? Why? Justify your answer. Use a social work example throughout your discussion.

17. Discuss why case-level evaluation designs are nothing more than interrupted time series group designs as presented in Chapter 12. Justify your answer. Use a social work example throughout your discussion.

GROUP EXERCISES

1. In groups of four, decide on a social work–related problem area. Derive an *exploratory* research question out of the problem area. Describe how you could carry out all three *exploratory-level* quantitative case-level evaluations (i.e., B, BC, BCD) that could answer your research question using any one of the data collection methods presented in Table 19.1. In your description, define and operationalize all relevant variables (e.g., independent, dependent, extraneous, intervening), the research question, potential rival hypotheses, the specific case-level evaluation design, the sample (research participants), the data collection method(s), and the data source(s) for each data collection method(s). Discuss the limitations

of your hypothetical studies. Present your discussion to the entire class.

2. In groups of four, repeat Exercise 1 using the two *descriptive* case-level evaluation designs (i.e., *AB, ABC*). Use a different data collection method and data source.

3. In groups of four, repeat Exercise 1 using the three *explanatory* case-level evaluation designs (i.e., *ABAB, BAB, BCBC*). Use a different data collection method and data source.

LIBRARY EXERCISES

1. At your university library, find a social work article that reports on a research study that used an *exploratory* case-level evaluation design. What do you feel the article contributed to the knowledge base of social work? Why? Justify your response. How could have this study been done using a "higher level" design?

2. Repeat Exercise 1 with a *descriptive* case-level evaluation design.

NOTES ON CHAPTER 23

_____

_____

_____

_____

_____

_____

_____

_____

_____

_____

_____

_____

_____

This chapter utilizes Study D

C h a p t e r   24

Program-Level Evaluation

CHAPTER OUTLINE

SELF-STUDY EXERCISES

1. Why do you believe that program-level evaluation is important to the social work profession? Explain in detail using the points as outlined in the chapter and provide examples from Study D

2. Discuss how program-level evaluations complement case-level evaluations (Chapter 23). Provide a social work example in your discussion.

3. After reading Chapters 3, and 24, discuss the various political factors that are associated with doing a program-level evaluation. Provide a social work example in your discussion.

4. After reading Chapters 2, and 24, discuss how a program-level evaluation can be an "applied" research study along with a "pure" research study. Provide a social work example in your discussion.

5. Discuss the various ways that a final report generated from a program-level evaluation can be useful to various stakeholder groups. Provide a social work example in your discussion.

6. Discuss some of the logistical problems that can occur when doing a program-level evaluation. Compare these problems with case-level evaluations. Provide a social work example in your discussion.

7. Discuss the various steps that you could use when anticipating logistical problems in a program-level evaluation. Compare these steps with the ones that you would use when doing a case-level evaluation. Provide a social work example in your discussion.

8. Discuss the differences between a formative program-level evaluation and a summative program-level evaluation. Compare and contrast these differences with "formative" case-level evaluations and "summative" case-level evaluations.

9. Discuss in detail how you would go about conducting a program-level evaluation that focuses on "outcome." Be specific in your discussion and utilize as many of the concepts as you can from the preceding chapters in this book. Some of these concepts would be: problem area, research question, conceptualization of problem area and research question, operationalization of the variables, sampling strategy, research design, data collection methods, data sources, generalization of findings, etc.

10. Discuss how a program-level evaluation is really an application (or applied research) of all the principles as contained in this book. Do the same for a case-level evaluation. Provide a social work example in your discussion.

11. Discuss how a program-level evaluation can use each one of the different data collection methods contained in Part V in this book (e.g., Table 19.1). Provide a social work example in your discussion.

12. Discuss how a program-level evaluation could use each one of the eight case-level evaluation designs as outlined in the previous chapter. Provide a social work example in your discussion.

GROUP EXERCISES

1. In groups of four, decide on a program-level evaluation question that deals with a program's effectiveness (research question or hypothesis). Describe how you could carry out a quantitative program-level evaluation that would answer your research question or hypothesis. In your description, define all relevant variables (e.g., independent, dependent, extraneous, intervening), the research question (or hypothesis), potential rival hypotheses, the specific research design, the sample (research participants), the data collection method(s), and the data source(s) for each data collection method(s). Discuss in detail how you would go about analyzing data generated from your study. Discuss the limitations of your hypothetical program-level evaluation. Present your discussion to the entire class.

2. With the same research question (or hypothesis) used in the above exercise, design a qualitative study and answer the same questions contained at the end of the exercise.

3. In groups of four, describe in detail how you would evaluate the effectiveness and efficiency of your social work program.

4. After reading Box 1.5, and in groups of four, discuss the various

cultural factors that need to be taken into account when doing a program-level evaluation. How are these factors different from the ones that need to be taken into account when doing a case-level evaluation? Discuss in detail and provide a social work example in your response. Report back to the entire class of what your group found.

LIBRARY EXERCISE

1. At your university library, locate a social work-relevant article that presents the results of a program evaluation. Evaluate the article using the contents of this entire book as a guide. How would you have done the study differently? Why? Be specific in your response.

NOTES ON CHAPTER 24

_____

_____

_____

_____

_____

_____

_____

_____

_____

_____

_____

_____

_____

_____

_____

C h a p t e r 25

Evaluation in Action

CHAPTER OUTLINE

SELF-STUDY EXERCISES

1. Discuss the various principles that underlie the design of case-level evaluations and program-level evaluations. Provide a social work example in your discussion.

2. List and discuss all of the stakeholders who may benefit from a case-level evaluation and a program-level evaluation. Provide a social work example in your discussion.

3. List and discuss all of the stakeholders who may benefit from an "effectiveness" program-level evaluation of your social work program. Be specific in your discussion.

4. What is case-level decision making? What is program-level decision making? How do the two levels of decision making complement one another? Provide one common social work example in your discussion.

5. What is the monitoring approach to evaluation? Provide a social work example in your discussion.

6. List and discuss some of the ethical considerations when doing case- and program-level evaluations. Provide one common social work example in your discussion.

7. Describe in detail the main differences between planned interventions and crisis interventions. Provide one common social work example in your discussion.

8. Discuss how you select research designs for case-level evaluations and form program-level evaluations. Provide one common social work example in your discussion.

GROUP EXERCISES

1. In groups of four, decide on a program-level evaluation question that deals with a program's effectiveness (research question or hypothesis). Describe how you could combine a *quantitative* case- **and** a

quantitative program-level evaluation at the same time that would answer your research question or hypothesis. In your description, define all relevant variables (e.g., independent, dependent, extraneous, intervening), the research question (or hypothesis), potential rival hypotheses, the specific research design, the sample (research participants), the data collection method(s), and the data source(s) for each data collection method(s). Discuss in detail how you would go about analyzing data generated from your study. Discuss the limitations of your hypothetical program-level evaluation. Present your discussion to the entire class.

2. With the same research question (or hypothesis) used in the above exercise, design a qualitative case-study evaluation and a quantitative program-level evaluation and answer the same questions contained at the end of the exercise. Repeat the exercise with a quantitative case-level evaluation and a qualitative program-level evaluation.

3. In groups of four, describe in detail how you would evaluate the effectiveness and efficiency of your social work program by combining case-level evaluations to form a program-level evaluation.

4. After reading Box 1.3, and in groups of four, discuss the various cultural factors that need to be taken into account when doing a program-level evaluation. How are these factors different from the ones that need to be taken into account when doing a case-level evaluation? Discuss in detail and provide a social work example in your response. Report back to the entire class what your group found.

LIBRARY EXERCISE

1. At your university library, locate a social work–relevant article that presents the combined results of a case-level and program-level evaluation. Evaluate the article using the contents of this entire book as a guide. How would you have done the study differently? Why? Be specific in your response.

NOTES ON CHAPTER 25

Sample Research Studies

John V. Flowers
Curtis D. Booarem

S t u d y   A

Four Studies Toward an Empirical Foundation for Group Therapy

THE DIFFICULTY OF OUTCOME EVALUATION in group therapy reflects a more complex version of the problem of psychotherapy evaluation in general. Since it has been demonstrated that using specific, operational outcome measures is more promising than global or personality assessment for measuring a single client's progress in therapy (Ciminero, Calhoun, & Adams, 1977; Mischel, 1977), it follows that situationally specific assessment is easier to accomplish when the group focuses on a single type of problem for all members. This is probably why the greatest proportion of research in "behavioral" group therapy has been with groups of clients with homogeneous problems (Upper & Ross, 1979, 1980, 1981).

Within groups of clients with heterogeneous problems, the most common assessment methods have been of a global or personality type (Strupp & Hadley, 1977, Bergin & Lambert, 1978). When more specific measures have been employed, the most common methods use the client or the therapist(s) to rate improvement on the problem(s) being addressed. Unfortunately, this form of assessment is unsound, since reliability is unknown and validity is unassessed and compromised by response bias.

Flowers and his associates (1981, 1980a, 1980b) have employed a modified (7 instead of 5 anchored points) version of Goal Attainment Scaling (GAS) to address situationally specific client goals without relying on client or therapist ratings (Kiresuk & Sherman, 1968). In this method of assessment, prior to the group session, clients write down problem disclosures that could be made in group and the name of one rater per problem outside the therapy group who could judge the client's progress on the goal of resolving this problem. In the next session the client can write down different potential problem disclosures, the same problem disclosures, or a mix. If the instructions were to write two problem disclosures prior to each group session, in sixteen weeks' duration, a client could write from two to 32 potential problem disclosures. Every problem actually disclosed in the therapy group becomes a client-selected goal for therapy, and never-disclosed problems become control goals. Both types of goals are rated by external raters unaware of goal type.

In this research, it has been shown that clients improve more on disclosed than never-disclosed problems, improve more on problem disclosures rated as higher than lower in intensity, and improve more on problem disclosures discussed in higher than lower cohesion sessions. While the GAS methodology employed in these studies potentially eliminates many of the problems that plague research on heterogeneous therapy groups, the goals (problem disclosures) were still client selected, and clients might have selected disclosures (therefore goals) that were going to improve because of factors other than group therapy.

The present paper reports the results of four studies. Study 1 addresses the methodological issue mentioned above to determine if client selection of disclosures biases the Goal Attainment Scaling methodology. In Study 1, instead of being client selected, the disclosures (and therefore the goals) were randomly selected for group disclosure and discussion. While this addresses the issue of selection bias, it still leaves the issues of actual group work unresolved. Even with randomly selected disclosures, any differential goal improvement could be because of the single act of disclosure rather than because of the subsequent group work done on the disclosure.

Study 2 addresses the issue of whether the amount of time spent working on a client's problem, or the frequency of positive and negative statements from other group members in such a discussion, affects client improvement. While these results partially answer the question of the effect of group work on client improvement, the variable of the client's emotional response and its change because of what other group members say is also an important factor in therapeutic change.

Study 3 addresses this question by inspecting what pattern of client emotional induction and reduction in group therapy maximizes client outcome.

While the first 3 studies help verify the GAS methodology and show its utility as a group outcome assessment method, the question of whether specific goal attainment relates to overall improvement remains open. The common method of employing specific measures along with some more standard personality measure to determine if there has also been "real," "general," or "more profound" changes as well (Bergin & Lambert, 1978) was not employed in these studies because it creates a theoretical polyglot and encourages the worst form of eclecticism.

If the overall importance of the specific client change is to be assessed, it must be measured by devices or methods that are theoretically consistent with the nature of the group process and the specific measures employed. The final study here reports the results of an attempt to devise a general assessment device based on the DSM III to assess overall change without theoretical bias. Such a general assessment device, if verified, would augment the more specific assessment techniques generally employed in behavioral group therapy.

STUDY 1

Method

Subjects on a waiting list for group therapy at a community clinic were contacted and asked if they would be willing to participate in a group with the following specific rules:

1. The group would meet for 1½ hours weekly for 16 weeks.
2. Clients would come to each group session group with two potential problem disclosures (numbered 1 and 2) written down with the name and address of a person outside the group who could rate the client's progress in resolving that problem.
3. The client agreed not to talk to any indicated rater about anything that happened in the group.

4. If the client was willing to talk during a session, one of the leaders would specify which problem to disclose (randomly chosen, 1 or 2), with the clear understanding that the other problem was not to be disclosed in that or subsequent sessions.

5. In subsequent sessions after a disclosure, the client could talk about the problem disclosed in a previous session or ask to talk about something new, which again required that two problem disclosures be written down, and that the problem discussed be chosen randomly.

Subjects

The subjects (3 males, 5 females) ranged in age from 23 to 41 (mean = 27.7). The first eight people contacted from the list all agreed to participate in the group and abide by the rules of disclosure. All subjects were guaranteed participation in another therapy group without the above restrictions if they finished the experimental group. All subjects finished the treatment attending an average of 14½ sessions each.

Therapists

The therapists were a male and female co-therapy team trained to conduct behavioral group therapy (Flowers & Schwartz, 1985).

Outcome Measures

Fifty different disclosures were made in the 16 group sessions. Two of these were on the not-to-disclose list, which eliminated both those disclosures and the previously paired disclosures from research consideration; therefore, 46 random disclosures and paired 46 never-disclosed problems with identified raters were employed in the outcome research. The external raters who had been identified were contacted within one week of the group's termination and were asked to rate the client's progress on the goal of resolving each disclosed and never-disclosed problem on a Likert type seven-point scale in the general form:

In terms of resolving the _____ problem, in the last 4 months (Client Name) is:

1. Much worse
2. Worse
3. Somewhat worse
4. Unchanged
5. Somewhat improved
6. Improved
7. Greatly improved

Ninety of the 92 goal assessments were returned.

Results

The 45 goals that had been randomly picked to be discussed in the therapy group were rated 5.34 compared to 4.48 for goals randomly selected never to be discussed (t (43) = 4.33, p < .001), indicating a significant client improvement even when the goal had been randomly selected to be discussed.

While Likert scales are commonly analyzed parametrically, the scale is not ratio; hence the same data were analyzed employing the Wilcoxon test to assure that the interval nature of the scale was not creating the significant difference (sum of positive pairs = 499, sum of negative pairs = 96, p < .001).

STUDY 2

Introduction

These results demonstrate that the differential improvement shown on the GAS between disclosed and never-disclosed problems (goals) occurs even when the disclosures are randomly elicited. This verifies that both previous and future differential results in more normally conducted groups, wherein the client can chose what to disclose, are not merely due to the client's choice of problem disclosures and goals. What this study does not resolve is whether it is merely disclosure, or the subsequent group work, that contributes to client improvement, which is the focus of Study 2.

Method

Subjects in three successive therapy groups at a community clinic volunteered and were studied for 10 one and one-half hour sessions. All subjects wrote two possible problem disclosures prior to each session, with the name of an outside rater who could assess the subject's progress on the goal of resolving the disclosed problem. A subject could disclose no problem, either problem, both problems, or a problem not written prior to the group in the session. If the disclosure was a problem not written prior to the group, it was written by the client after the session.

Subjects

Twenty-three subjects (10 male, 13 female) ranging in age from 19 to 44 years (mean = 27.2) completed the experimental group sessions.

Therapists

The therapists were three male and female co-therapy teams trained to conduct behavioral group therapy (Flowers & Schwartz, 1985).

Outcome Measures

The first two sessions in each group were used to train the judges (graduate students in a practicum class who were not yet qualified to see clients) who collected data for the next eight sessions. Three judges independently assessed (and signaled with an arrow that could point to "on goal" or "off goal" and another arrow that pointed to a client name) whether the group was discussing a client goal (i.e., talking about a disclosure the client had made). A fourth judge recorded the time the group spent discussing the problem when two of the three judges agreed that the group was discussing a specific client's goal. A fifth and sixth judge recorded the frequency of positive and negative statements made by all group members except the client while the timer was on (Flowers, Booarem, Brown, & Harris, 1974). All judges observed the group through a one-way mirror. At the end of the ten sessions, a goal list of discussed and never-discussed problems was made for each client along with the outside raters the clients had indicated could rate any improvement on the goal. These external raters were then contacted to rate the clients' progress on the goals.

Results

Of 2160 scheduled minutes, 2040 actually occurred. In the 2040 potential minutes, at least two judges agreed that 1666 were spent discussing a specific client's goals that were eventually rated by the external raters. Of the 74 goals that were discussed in the 24 sessions (3 groups times 8 sessions each), 72 had external raters specified and 68 ratings were returned by external raters (mean = 5.48). The improvement on the 68 client goals correlated significantly ($r = .32, p < .001$) with the time spent discussing each goal.

In a separate analysis, the improvement on the 68 discussed and rated goals correlated significantly ($r = .68, p < .001$) with the frequency of positive plus negative statements per minute as rated by the fifth and sixth judges. The frequency of positive and negative statements per minute per goal was calculated and varied from .20 to 2.91. The 34 goals with the lowest positive plus negative rating per minute (intensity) were rated at an improvement rate of 4.76 compared to 6.18 for the 34 goals with the highest intensity ($t (66) = 5.39, p < .001$). An ANOVA of goal improvement by group was not significant ($F (2,65) = 18$) demonstrating that the 3 groups were equivalent in terms of this measure of client improvement.

STUDY 3

Introduction

This study demonstrates that client improvement is not merely due to the client disclosing the problem (and the therapeutic goal) but is positively influenced by the amount of time spent in group work, and is more influenced by what might be called the "intensity" of the discussion. While the frequency of emotional statements made by other group members during a discussion correlates with the client change on what was discussed, this does not assess any differential response of the client during the group work. Instead of the "intensity" of the discussion, Study 3 assesses the effect of the client's emotionality during the discussion on outcome.

Method

In Part 1 of this study, clients in three separate therapy groups at a community clinic completed 16 one and one-half hour sessions. After the session, each member wrote down a brief version of what he or she had disclosed in the session and indicated a rater as in the previous studies. All the group members and therapists rated each disclosed problem on a seven-point Likert-type scale:

1. No emotion evidenced
2. Very little emotion evidenced
3. Little emotion evidenced
4. Some emotion evidenced
5. Moderate emotion evidenced
6. Considerable emotion evidenced
7. A great deal of emotion evidenced

Each problem was rated for the highest emotion level reached by the discloser during the problem discussion and the subsequent lowest level the discloser reached prior to the end of that group session. The reason that reduction can be rated after the problem discussion is completed is that groups often return to disclosing members late in the group to assess how they are feeling. Every disclosed problem was given an emotional induction-reduction score based on the mean difference over all ratings (other clients and therapists) between the highest and lowest level of emotion rated during the problem discussion. After the termination of therapy, the outside raters were contacted for ratings in the previous study.

In Part 2, clients in a therapy group completed 16 sessions of 1.5 hour duration. Prior to the group session the therapists were given a random number list that instructed them to attempt to either induce or abort emotional induction of each problem as it was disclosed. In all cases where emotionality was induced, whether by therapist design or not, maximum reduction was always attempted during the session. Thus, the therapists attempted to randomly generate a set of discussed problem disclosures which had either (1) a maximum difference between the highest and subsequent lowest level of emotionality (obtained by inducing maximum emotion and subsequently reducing it to minimum levels), or (2) a minimum of such difference (obtained by inducing minimum emotion). The same data as above were collected. The group members were unaware of the independent variable.

Subjects

In Part 1, 23 subjects (14 female and 9 male) of ages ranging from 21 to 56 years (mean = 32.4) completed the 16 group sessions.

In Part 2, 8 subjects (4 male and 4 female) of ages ranging from 23 to 35 (mean = 25.6) completed the 16 group sessions.

Therapists

The therapists were four male and female co-therapy teams trained to conduct behavioral group therapy (Flowers & Schwartz, 1985).

Outcome Measures

In Part 1 of this study, of the 93 problem disclosures that had potential external raters, 86 ratings of goal improvement were returned by mail.

These goals were given an emotional difference rating based on the mean difference between high and low emotionality ratings by the group members and leaders during that goals discussion.

In Part 2, 50 separable problem disclosures were actually made to the group, of which the therapists were successful in keeping the problem disclosure in the correct predetermined category of emotional induction (mean rating of 4 or below for low induction, 5 or above for high induction) in 43 cases. Seven problem disclosures were made that could not be induced (4) or could not be held to low emotional induction (3).

Results

In Part 1, the 43 goals with the highest emotional induction-reduction difference were rated at 5.59 compared to 4.63 for the low emotional induction-reduction goals ($t (84) = 3.86, p < .001$).

In Part 2, of 43 disclosed goals, 31 had external raters and 27 ratings were returned. One goal was discarded randomly to achieve the even number of goals necessary for a split half procedure, and the 13 with the highest emotional induction were given external ratings of 5.67 compared to 4.85 for the 13 with the lowest emotional induction ($t (24) = 2.98, p < .01$).

STUDY 4

Introduction

While the previous three studies demonstrate the efficacy of the GAS methodology for assessing specific outcome in heterogeneous client groups, they do not demonstrate that improvement on specific therapeutic goals is related to overall client improvement. As previously stated, this is not an easily resolved assessment question. Most measures of overall improvement are both theory specific and inconsistent with the specific problem approach of behavioral group therapy. Study 4 is devoted to testing the reliability and concurrent validity of a general measure of client improvement based on the DSM III as well as testing if specific outcome results are paralleled by more generalized results.

Specifically, clients in three therapy groups were assessed both on the GAS methodology and on a more general measure derived from the DSM III.

Method

Persons in three successive therapy groups at a community clinic were subjects for this study. Each subject understood that he or she would undergo four hours of individual counseling to prepare for group therapy, 24 one and one-half hour sessions of group therapy, and 4 hours of individual counseling at the end of the group to determine if more group therapy was appropriate. All subjects wrote two potential problem disclosures on a card prior to each group therapy meeting as in the previous studies. At the end of the 24 sessions a goal list of discussed and never-discussed problems was made for each client along with the raters the clients had indicated as potential judges who were contacted for their ratings after the termination of the therapy groups.

Subjects

Of the 27 subjects initially assigned to the three groups, 24 (9 male, 15 female) of ages ranging from 17 to 49 years (mean = 29.4) completed the group and individual sessions.

Outcome Measures

Thirteen therapists (none of whom conducted the group sessions) conducted the initial four individual therapy sessions and were in fact determining the client's appropriateness for group. These therapists filled out an 80-item DSM III questionnaire on each client designed by the first author on the basis of research by McDowell (1982) and Nicolette (1982).

Fifteen therapists (none of whom had conducted the group sessions) conducted the four postgroup individual sessions after group and were in fact determining the clients' continued need for group therapy. All therapists filled the same 80-item DSM III questionnaire used by the pregroup therapists and were led to believe the research was a diagnostic reliability study, which was in fact going on at the clinic concurrently with the present research.

At the end of group therapy, one of the group therapists was randomly selected to fill out the same DSM III diagnostic questionnaire on each client. The other therapist in each group filled out the DSM III questionnaire twice, with the instruction to generate both the most optimistic and most pessimistic reasonable assessment of the client. Both therapists knew these data were to be used to evaluate the group's effectiveness.

The numerical answer (1 to 5) to each of the 80 questions on each client was entered into a computer program designed by the first author. This program yields a list of all DSM III diagnoses that might describe this client's problems and indicates if there is substantial or merely provisional evidence for each possible diagnosis. Thus, each of the 24 subjects received a full, computer-run DSM III diagnosis before group therapy and received four such diagnoses after the group terminated.

Client goals discussed and never discussed were sent to the indicated external raters as in the previous studies.

Results

Concurrent Validity

Prior to group therapy the 24 subjects (24 computer runs) had a total of 35 DSM III diagnoses rated as substantial, or 1.46 each. After group therapy, the 24 subjects' computer-run tests yielded 20 DSM III diagnoses rated as substantial, or .83 each (t (23) = 4.73, p < .001). Thus, the individual independent therapists rated the subject as significantly less pathological after group therapy than before.

Since some of the diagnoses for which there was substantial evidence prior to group therapy became diagnoses for which there was provisional evidence after therapy, a second analysis was conducted in which each subject was given two pathology points for any substantial diagnosis and one point for any diagnosis for which there was some evidence. Prior to group therapy the 24 subjects had an average of 4.04 pathology points each, compared to 2.71 after group therapy (t (23) = 7.52, p < .001). Since these data are clearly not interval in nature, the same data were analyzed by a Wilcoxon test to determine if the results were created by a violation of the parametric assumptions. The results (sum of positive ranks = 268.5, sum of negative ranks = 7.5, $p > .001$) clearly indicated that the significant differences in pathology before and after the therapy group were not a result of a violation of parametric assumptions.

Of 127 disclosures made in group, 123 had external raters and of 106 never made, 101 had raters indicated. These were sent to the raters with a return rate of 115 disclosures made and 91 never made. Problems discussed in the group were rated with greater improvement (mean = 5.57) than the goals never discussed (mean = 4.65, $t(204) = 5.82$, $p < .001$). To be certain the results were not due to the noninterval aspect of the Likert scale, the same data were analyzed with a Mann-Whitney. These results were a $U1 = 2910.5$ and $U2 = 7554.5$, $z = 4.56$, $p < .001$, indicating that the results were not due to the nonparametric nature of the Likert type scale rating used.

Reliability

The 24 subjects were evaluated as having .46 substantial diagnoses each by the group therapists who filled out a single assessment, making the most accurate diagnosis they could. This was significantly different ($t(23) = 3.19$, $p < .001$) from the evaluation given by the subsequent individual therapists (.83). These results indicate that the group therapists who had worked with the clients perceived them as significantly less pathological than the subsequent individual therapists.

The same 24 subjects were rated at means of .71 substantial diagnoses when this rating was derived from the average of the most optimistic and pessimistic evaluation from the other three group therapists. These results are not significantly different from the subsequent evaluations of the individual therapists (0–83). Thus, when the group leader is asked to give a range of pathology rather than give a single point estimate, the middle of this range is closer to another independent therapist's judgment of the client's present functioning than is the group leader's best estimate.

DISCUSSION

The use of client disclosures in the therapy group as goals in a Goal Attainment Scaling (GAS) assessment procedure makes the GAS method extremely easy to use in group therapy research. The use of client-specified raters, unaware of what goals have and have not been therapeutically addressed, eliminates the potential biasing effect of a rater wishing the intervention to be shown effective or ineffective. The present study strongly suggests that client selection of the goal to be assessed does not affect the outcome and suggests that this method of assessment of client outcome measures primarily the effect of the therapy group on client change. While there can still be response bias, it biases both experimental and control goals, thus should not yield false positive results.

This methodology provides an alternative to random assignment and control groups in the design of clinical research when the more traditional experimental control is difficult or impossible. The use of control goals rather than control groups means that every subject, in a sense, is part of a simplified multiple baseline design that is not limited to clearly observable units of behavior. This is not to say that every problem of assessment has been or even can be resolved by this method. Not all goals can have raters, raters are not equally reliable, and the reliability is presently unknown.

Studies 2 and 3 use this methodology to inspect other aspects of group therapy. Study 2 demonstrates that both the time spent discussing the disclosure and intensity (number of positive and negative statements by other members) during the group work significantly affect the outcome. The fact that intensity is a more powerful agent than time spent is both seductive and dangerous.

Simply increasing intensity could lead to group casualties just as easily as it could increase positive outcome (Lieberman, Yalom & Miles, 1973; Flowers, Booarem, & Seacat, 1974). Positive change is not induced by merely increasing group session intensity, but by increasing intensity within a safe context, Specifically, intensity as measured here is made up of both positive and negative statements, not merely negative ("encounter") statements that are too prevalent in some group work.

Study 3 begins the process of investigating the variables involved in making the intensity factor work safely. Both positive and negative statements induce emotion and while emotional induction motivates change, the present study demonstrates it is the difference between emotional induction and emotional reduction that leads to positive outcome in group therapy. Clients who leave the group in a state of emotional induction without subsequent reduction may be prime candidates for change in a negative direction, i.e., casualty status. The work of Lieberman, Yalom and Miles (1973) suggests, that such unsafe induction may be because of an overabundance or overintensity of negative messages in the group session. This area should be addressed in future research to clearly determine what is safe and unsafe group practice.

The results of the final study replicate the results of previous work, i.e., behavioral group therapy works on the specific goals addressed in the therapy. However, this study also indicates that these results are also paralleled by the more general result of less overall pathology, strengthening the case for the significance, as well as the validity, of the results. This DSM III method of assessment is based on the assumption that pathology is reflected in diagnosis and that client improvement is indicated when a diagnosis that was a possibility is removed in the course of therapy. This assumption and therefore the assessment methodology will be weakened when the pathology is not reflected in diagnosis as in cases of family system pathology, or not necessarily reflected in individual disorders such as in low social skills. It would also be weakened in cases of confused rather than generally severe disorders; however most highly confusing disorders (e.g., Bipolar, Borderline) are also severe, nevertheless, this methodology would have to be independently verified as a general measure of improvement in such cases.

The evaluations of the group therapists under two different sets of instructions (optimistic and pessimistic) indicate that an even easier method than that employed in this study may be possible in future research. The group therapists (one per group) instructed to fill out the 80-item questionnaire to make the most accurate diagnosis, knowing that the rating was to be used to assess the group's effectiveness, evaluated the clients as less pathological than the subsequent therapists, who thought the evaluation was part of a diagnostic reliability study. This seems to be yet another example of therapist bias in the direction of self-interest in outcome evaluation.

On the other hand, when the other therapist in each group was asked to fill out two questionnaires on each client—one indicating the most optimistic and one indicating the most pessimistic pathological possibilities—the average of the number of DSM III diagnoses produced by these two ratings was almost identical to the subsequent evaluations of the presumably less biased individual therapists. Thus, the evaluation of global improvement may be able to be done by the therapist, provided he or she is asking the right questions—i.e., the range of pathology possible rather than the best assessment of the client's present status.

The use of the DSM III as the global measure of client improvement in group therapy (or any therapy for that matter) has a number of advantages. First, unlike other global measures, the DSM III method is not linked to a single theory of therapy. This method addresses pathology rather than personality and can be used with any other method of specific assessment. Additionally, the method employs a universal language that is understandable by therapists of any persuasion. Finally, the present method of assessment is sensitive enough to reflect changes brought about by group therapeutic intervention. At present, the DSM III outcome assessment method suffers from some of the same limitations that the DSM III itself suffers; it is limited in showing systems changes (i.e., marital or family) that are not also indicated by changes in individual pathology, and it may give falsely high pathology scores in diagnostically confusing cases.

REFERENCES

Bergin, A.E., & Lambert, M.J. (1978). The evaluation of therapeutic outcomes. In S.L. Garfield & A.E. Bergin (Eds.), *Handbook of psychotherapy and behavior change: An empirical analysis*. New York: Wiley.

Ciminero, A.R., Calhoun, K.S., & Adams, H.E. (1977). *Handbook of behavioral assessment*. New York: Wiley.

Flowers, J.V., Booarem, C.D., Brown, T.R., & Harris, D. (1974). An investigation of a technique for facilitating patient to patient therapeutic interactions in group therapy. *Journal of Community Psychology, 2,* 39-42.

Flowers, J.V., Booarem, C.D., & Hartman, K.A. (1981). Client improvement on higher and lower intensity problems as a function of group cohesiveness. *Psychotherapy: Theory, Research, and Practice, 18,* 246-251.

Flowers, J.V., Booarem, C.D., & Seacat, G. (1974). The effect of positive and negative feedback on members' sensitivity to other members in group therapy. *Psychotherapy: Theory, Research, and Practice, 11,* 346-350.

Flowers, J.V., Hartman, K.A., Mann, R.J., Kidder, S., & Booarem, C.D. (1980). The effects of group cohesion and client flexibility on therapy outcome. In D. Upper & S.M. Ross, (Eds.). *Behavioral group therapy, 1980.* Champaign, IL: Research Press.

Flowers, J.V., & Schwartz, B. (1985). Behavioral group therapy with clients with homogeneous problems. In S.M. Ross & D. Upper (Eds.), *Handbook of behavioral group therapy.* New York: Plenum Press.

Flowers, J.V., Tapper, B., Kidder, S., Wein, G., & Booarem, C.D. (1980). Generalization and maintenance of client outcome in group therapy. In D. Upper & S.M. Ross (Eds.), *Behavioral group therapy, 1980.* Champaign, IL: Research Press.

Kiresuk, T.J., & Sherman, R.E. (1968). Goal attainment scaling: A general method for evaluating comprehensive community mental health programs. *Community Mental Health Journal, 17,* 443-453.

Lieberman, M.A., Yalom, I.D., & Miles, M.B. (1973). *Encounter group: First facts.* New York: Basic Books.

McDowell, D.J. (1982). *Psychiatric diagnosis: Rater reliability and prediction using "psychological rating scale for diagnostic classification."* Unpublished Doctoral Dissertation. Denton, TX: North Texas State University.

Mischel, W. (1977). On the future of personality research. *American Psychologist, 32,* 246-254.

Nicolette, M. (1982). *Interrater reliability of the psychological scale for diagnostic classification.* Unpublished Masters Thesis. Denton, TX: North Texas State University.

Strupp, H.H. (1978). Psychotherapy research and practice: An overview. In S.L. Garfield & A.E. Bergin (Eds.), *Handbook of psychotherapy and behavior change: An empirical analysis.* New York: Wiley.

Strupp, H.H., & Hadley, S.W. (1977). A tripartite model of mental health and therapeutic outcomes. *American Psychologist, 32,* 187-196.

Upper, D., & Ross, S.M. (1979). *Behavioral group therapy, 1979.* Champaign, IL: Research Press.

Upper, D., & Ross, S.M. (1980). *Behavioral group therapy, 1980.* Campaign, IL: Research Press.

Upper, D., & Ross, S.M. (1981). *Behavioral group therapy, 1981.* Champaign, IL: Research Press.

James R. Moran

S t u d y   B

Social Work Education and Students' Humanistic Attitudes

SOCIAL WORK IS BASED on humanitarian ideals. The social work code of ethics calls for belief in the dignity of human beings, respect for individual differences, and a commitment to improving the general welfare (Lemmon, 1983). Professional social work education must be concerned with both the knowledge and the value base of social work (Koerin, 1977). Consequently, social work educators seek to shape students' attitudes so as to develop a commitment to strive for individual and institutional arrangements that will have a humanistic impact on clients (Howard & Flaitz, 1982).

Concern with values and attitudes may be even more important in the future, as social workers are forced to deal with cutbacks in social programs and a public that is less than enthusiastic about raising taxes to support the needy. It thus is important that social work educators evaluate their impact on values and attitudes. The study reported in this paper examined the relationship between undergraduate social work education and the humanistic attitudes of social work students.

Previous research into the relationship between social work education and values/attitudes has produced contradictory results. A comparison of beginning and graduating MSW students' attitudes toward equal rights and commitment to service found no significant differences in attitude between those who had finished their studies and those who had not (Varley, 1963). Cyrns (1977) found that social work graduate students actually had more negative attitudes toward human nature and the causes of poverty than did social work undergraduate students. Two longitudinal studies reported positive, but statistically non-significant, changes in attitudes toward equal rights when comparing MSW students at the beginning and end of their education (Varley, 1963; Judah, 1979). However, Sharwell (1974) found a significant positive change in graduate social work students' attitudes on such issues as the extensiveness of public assistance programs and the effect of programs on recipients' motivation to work. Finally, a study of undergraduate social work education showed a significant positive relationship between the number of social work courses completed and attitudes toward persons on public assistance (Merdinger, 1982).

The study reported here differs from most of the previous research: It focuses entirely on undergraduate social work students. It also attempts to control for several factors likely to be related to the students' attitudes. The study is based on the premise that students who have completed more social work courses will have more humanistic attitudes than will students who have completed fewer courses.

METHODOLOGY

A cross-sectional sample was used for this research. The setting was an accredited baccalaureate program located within a southeastern state university of approximately 14,000 students. The sampling frame consisted of all 275 students enrolled in social work courses during Spring semester 1985. A random sample of 150 was drawn from this universe. In order to ensure adequate variability in the number of social work courses completed, the sample was stratified on the basis of enrollment in lower or upper division courses; one half of the sample was selected from each level.

Subjects were requested to complete a questionnaire that collected demographic data and specific details about the social work courses they had completed. The instrument also measured the students' humanistic attitudes. The questionnaire was distributed by faculty during class periods with the request that it be completed outside of class and be returned at the next class meeting. In addition to the questionnaire, the respondents were provided with an informed consent statement that explained the general purpose of the study and guaranteed confidentiality.

Of the 150 students in the sample, 112 returned completed questionnaires. Of those who did not take part, seven stated that they did not want to participate; the other 31 simply did not return the questionnaire or the consent form. To assess the degree that those who responded were representative of the total sample, the gender and race of the respondents and all majors in the Social Work department were compared. Respondents were 71.4 percent female and 26.8 percent nonwhite, while all majors were 65.5 percent female and 22.9 percent nonwhite. While this certainly does not eliminate the possibility of selection bias, it does indicate some degree of representativeness on the part of the sample.

Students' humanistic attitudes were assessed with the Social Humanistic Ideology Scale. This scale measures attitudes about human nature, social justice, human rights, and individual freedom. The authors of the scale report the alpha reliability coefficients for these subscales at .68, .76, .48, and .64, respectively. They also indicate the study's content validity (Howard & Flaitz, 1982).

Only the two subscales with the highest reliability coefficients were used for this study. The "human nature" section of the instrument examines perceptions of the needs and motivations of clients of social service programs. It also examines respondents' perceptions of the role that individual pathology plays in economic success or failure. The "social justice" subscale assesses attitudes about the fairness in the distribution of life-sustaining resources. Specific items deal with the use of social action to achieve a more just society, economic reform, and efforts to redress past injustices against members of minority groups. Both subscales consisted of ten statements to which students were asked to respond by checking one of five options. The choices varied from strongly agree to strongly disagree. Each item received a score from 1 to 5; higher scores indicated stronger identification with humanistic attitudes. Thus, the possible range of scores for each subscale was from a low of 10 to a high of 50.

Students were asked to list the number of social work courses they had completed to date. Since the data were collected at the end of the semester, courses in which students then were enrolled were considered completed courses. Additional data were collected on respondents' age, gender, and race.

Table B-1   Correlation Coefficients

Variables	Age	Male	Non-white	Social Justice	Human Nature
Number of Social					
Work Courses	.1530	-.0415	.0539	.0900	.3395*
Age		.0548	-.0706	-.1692	-.1522
Male			-.0638	-.1827	-.1950
Nonwhite				.2870	.0292
Social Justice					.3954*

* = Significant at $p < .05$

Regression analysis examined the relationship between humanistic attitudes and social work education. Two separate dependent variables were utilized in the analysis. They were the scores from the human nature and social justice subscales.

The primary independent variable was the number of social work courses completed by the respondents. Age, gender, and race also were treated as independent variables in the regression models. Age was measured in years. Gender was represented by a dummy variable with a value of 1 for male and 0 for female. Race was represented by a dummy variable with a value of 1 for nonwhite and 0 for white. This approach allowed the influence of age, gender, and race to be controlled while examining the primary relationship of interest.

RESULTS

The scores on the human nature subscale varied from a low of 18 to a high of 45 with a mean score of 32. The social justice scores varied from 22 to 45 with a mean score of 32.5. The number of social work courses completed by the respondents varied from 1 to 9 with a mean of 4.08. The age of the students varied from 18 to 59 with a mean of 22.2 years. There were 32 male respondents and 80 female respondents. The racial composition of the group was 82 whites and 30 nonwhites.

Table B-1 presents the zero-order correlation coefficients for the variables used in the regression models. These results show the relationship between social work education and students' humanistic attitudes. There was a statistically significant and positive relationship between the number of social work courses completed and attitudes concerning human nature. However, the correlation between the number of courses and attitudes concerning social justice was not statistically significant. Table B-1 also shows that there is no significant association between the four independent variables. This is important because regression analysis attempts to examine the relationship between the dependent variable and each of the independent variables, while controlling for the effects of the other variables in the model. For example, the relationship between humanistic attitudes and social work education can be looked at while holding the effects of age, gender and race constant. The lack of strong correlations between the independent variables indicates that regression analysis is an appropriate procedure by which to attempt to evaluate their independent effects.

Table B-2 and Table B-3 display the results for the two regression models. The explanatory power of the equations was poor, with only 17.7 percent of the variance in the human nature score explained and 15.7 percent of the variance explained for the social justice score. The adjusted R^2s for the human nature and social justice models were .142 and .123, respectively. This means that when adjusted for sample size and the number of independent variables, the models explain even less of the variance. However, an examination of the residuals plotted against the predicted values and each independent variable revealed no pattern of nonrandomness. In addition, histograms of the residuals were essentially normal. Thus, although the models explain little of the variance, there appears to be no violation of the basic assumptions of regression analysis.

Statistical significance was obtained for two variables in the human nature equation, but for only one in the social justice model. The number of completed social work courses had a statistically significant ($p = .0003$) and positive relationship with the score on the subscale for human nature, but was not statistically significant in the social justice equation. Age had a significant ($p = .0485$) negative relationship with the human nature score and negative but nonsig-nificant relationship to the social justice score. As indicated by the male dummy variable results, gender had a nonsignificant relationship to both human nature and social justice. Race, as represented by the dummy variable for nonwhite, had a statistically significant ($p = .0013$) and positive relationship to the social justice score—it was not statistically significant in the human nature model.

The standardized coefficients (betas) show the relative importance of the independent variables in the models. The social work courses variable had the largest standardized coefficient in the human nature equation while the variable for nonwhite had the largest in the social justice model.

Table B-2   Regression Results for Human Nature
                       Subscale (N = 99)

Variables	Coefficient	Standard Error	BETA	t-test	p
Number of Social					
Work Courses	.8098	.2159	.3569	3.75	.0003
Age	-.2325	.1163	-.1978	-1.99	.0485
Male	-2.1713	1.2469	-.1643	-1.74	.0849
Nonwhite	.0382	1.2000	.0030	.03	.9747
Constant	34.3161				

$$R^2 = .177 \quad f = 5.039$$
$$\text{Adjusted } R^2 = .142 \quad p = .0010$$

DISCUSSION

Although the coefficient for age was statistically significant only in the human nature equation, its negative direction in both of the models is important. It was noted earlier that several studies found a negative relationship between social work education and student attitudes. However, none of these studies attempted to control for the influence of age. If the negative relationship between age and attitudes also was present in past research, it would provide a partial explanation for some of the contradictions in the findings. This may be especially true in studies comparing undergraduate and graduate students. While not

Table B-3   Regression Results for Social Justice
                       Subscale (N = 103)

Variables	Coefficient	Standard Error	BETA	t-test	p
Number of Social					
Work Courses	.2361	.1949	.1145	1.21	.2287
Age	-.1690	.1073	-.1486	-1.58	.1184
Male	-1.5087	1.1024	-.1274	-1.37	.1743
Nonwhite	3.5355	1.0665	.3091	3.32	.0013
Constant	34.8337				

$$R^2 = .157 \quad f = 4.562$$
$$\text{Adjusted } R^2 = .123 \quad p = .0020$$

conclusive, it suggests that we may need to pay particular attention to older students when addressing issues related to social work values and attitudes.

Although the author had no *a priori* expectation about the role of race in the models, the results for the nonwhite variable require closer examination. This variable had the smallest beta coefficient and did not achieve statistical significance in the human nature equation. However, in the social justice model it had the largest beta coefficient and was the only statistically significant variable. In other words, nonwhites scored higher than whites on the social justice subscale, but essentially were no different on the human nature subscale. A partial explanation for this finding may exist in the specified items on the social justice subscale. Out of the ten items, two related directly to issues of redressing injustices to minority groups, while the other eight dealt primarily with issues related to reducing poverty. Because of the high rates of poverty and economic deprivation faced by nonwhites, it seems likely that nonwhite respondents would be more inclined to feel strongly about these particular items. In other words, the findings on race may be due to the construction of the particular subscale rather than offer any evidence that nonwhites are more concerned with social justice than whites are.

The most surprising finding was that the number of social work courses had a positive relationship with attitudes about human nature, but essentially no relationship to the students' attitudes toward social justice. Entering the variables singly into the models showed that the number of courses explained 10.7 percent of the variance in the score for human nature but only 1.4 percent of the variance in the score for social justice. Similarly, the standardized regression coefficient for this variable was almost twice as large as any of the others in the human nature equation, but was the smallest coefficient in the social justice model.

There are several possible explanations for this finding. First, the social work curriculum may stress issues of human nature more than issues of social justice. Second, students may start the program with more positive attitudes toward issues of social justice and hence change may be less likely. Third, it is possible that students' attitudes toward human nature are more easily influenced than their attitudes towards social justice are. There also may be an interaction between these three possibilities and other explanations not mentioned. The data permit tentative examination of the first two alternatives.

While a content analysis of each course would be necessary to thoroughly explore the issue of the curriculum's focus, an overall impression can be gained by examining the general content and titles of the nine social work courses. It appears that the programs' curriculum is balanced between courses that tend to emphasize individual issues and those that emphasize social issues. There does not seem to be a lack of courses that normally deal with issues of social justice. For example, three of the nine courses cover history and social policy issues, while a fourth course deals with the organization of social welfare systems. Clearly no firm conclusion can be drawn without a detailed analysis of each course's content. However, the general focus of the courses casts doubt on the argument that the curriculum favors material dealing with human nature over material reflecting issues of social justice.

The second alternative can be examined through a comparison of mean scores on the two subscales. Although the regression results show that the number of completed social work courses has a positive relationship to the human nature score and essentially no relationship to the social justice score, the overall means are roughly equal at 32.0 and 32.5, respectively. This suggests that the social justice score must be higher than the human nature score for students beginning the program. In this study, students who had completed only one social work course had mean scores of 29.9 for the human nature scale and 32.8 for the social justice scale. This indicates that the students had to make greater changes in their attitudes about human nature than in their attitudes about social justice and thus may have been more susceptible to the education process along this dimension. However, the low initial scores on human nature raise the alternative explanation that the change was simply regression to the mean rather than the result of the number of social work courses completed.

Although the findings of this study are important, there are several limitations. One of these is the cross-sectional approach used in this research. Comparing different students at various points in the educational process opens the possibility that any observed differences in their attitudes may be the result of differences between the students rather than the influence of the social work courses completed. The small sample size is another limitation and perhaps is related to the lack of variance explained by the regression models. Furthermore, only one undergraduate social work program was examined. This program may not be representative of social work programs in general. In addition, it is possible that the particular geographical location of the program biased the results in some manner. Thus, this study may be limited in its external validity.

CONCLUSION

This research study lends partial support to the hypothesis that the number of completed social work courses is positively related to students' humanistic attitudes. Furthermore, it appears that social work education has a stronger influence on attitudes about human nature than on those about social justice. This tentative finding may suggest that students start the program with more positive attitudes about social justice than about issues related to human nature, thus making change in the former set of attitudes less likely.

It is important to note that this research merely examined the situation as it is, rather than what may be possible. In other words, looking at the impact of the number of social work courses completed is only one way of examining the relationship between social work education and attitudes. Further research is needed on the manner in which social work educators attempt to influence values and attitudes. It is possible that particular methods may work better with some attitudes than with others. For example, it may be found that discussion may best influence attitudes about issues such as human nature whereas an action-oriented or experiential approach is needed to affect attitudes concerning social justice. There also is a need for research that examines the relationship between attitudes and actions. Changing attitudes is an important first step, however. Effective social work practice demands that humanistic attitudes become translated into action. The exploration of these issues is critical if social work education is to meet its mandate of producing practitioners committed to our code of ethics and who are willing to work for the improvement of the general welfare.

REFERENCES

Cyrns, A.G. (1977). Social work education and student ideology: A multivariate study of professional socialization. *Journal of Education for Social Work, 13,* 44-51.

Howard, T.U., & Flaitz, J. (1982). A scale to measure humanistic attitudes of social work students. *Social Work Research and Abstracts, 18,* 11-18.

Judah, E.H. (1979). Values: The uncertain component in social work. *Journal of Education for Social Work, 15,* 79-86.

Koerin, B. (1977). Values in social work education: Implications for baccalaureate degree programs. *Journal of Education for Social Work, 13,* 84-90.

Lemmon, J.A. (1983). Legal issues and ethical codes. In A. Rosenblatt & D. Waldfogel (Eds.), *Handbook of clinical work* (pp. 853-865). San Francisco, CA: Jossey-Bass.

Merdinger, J.M. (1982). Socialization into a profession: The case of undergraduate social work students. *Journal of Education for Social Work, 18,* 12-19.

Sharwell, G.R. (1974). Can values be taught? A study of two variables related to orientation of social work graduate students toward public dependency. *Journal of Education for Social Work, 10,* 99-105.

Varley, B.K. (1963). Socialization in social work education. *Social Work, 8,* 102-109.

Michael W. Stephens
Richard M. Grinnell, Jr.
Judy L. Krysik

S t u d y   C

Victims of Child Sexual Abuse: A Research Note

CHILD SEXUAL ABUSE is not a recent phenomenon and has received considerable attention over the years (e.g., Howes, 1986; Sgroi, 1982). Indeed, child sexual abuse has been occurring for quite some time (e.g., Finkelhor & Hotaling, 1984; Howes, 1986; Russell, 1983). The most recent data of the American Humane Association (Russell & Trainor, 1984) report an increase in the number of reported cases across the United States. In a six-year period from 1976 to 1982 there was an increase in the number of reported cases from 1,975 to 22,918. At the present time similar national data are not available for Canada.

One of the reasons for an increase in reporting may be a loosening of the operational definition of child sexual abuse. Historically, the meaning attached to child sexual abuse was only incest that involved sexual intercourse. In fact, the terms "child sexual abuse" and "incest" were often used interchangeably (Faria & Belohlavek, 1984).

Over the years, various authors have defined child sexual abuse along a range from a narrow extreme to a more open, less restrictive definition (e.g., Giaretto, 1982; Sgroi, 1982; Wyatt & Peters, 1986).

PURPOSE OF STUDY

The rising incidence of child sexual abuse poses many social work practice and research questions. One of the greatest concerns of child care workers today is that of the victim. The focus of this study was on the variables related to the victim in an attempt to present Canadian-based data about the victims of child sexual abuse.

METHODOLOGY

The Setting

In Canada, child welfare is a provincially legislated responsibility. In Alberta, the Province of Alberta Child Welfare Act was passed by the Alberta Legislature on May 31, 1984, and proclaimed on July 1, 1985. This act forms the basis for child welfare intervention in Alberta. The Ministry that administers the child welfare legislation for the province is Alberta Social Services. Any allegation of child sexual abuse must be referred to Alberta Social Services for investigation purposes.

The delivery of child welfare services in Alberta occurs through a decentralized system located in six geographic regions. This study was carried out in one of Alberta's largest regions, which includes a large metropolitan city and the surrounding rural territory. Five geographic offices offer an investigation/intake program within the region.

Operational Definition

To be consistent with the study's setting, we adopted the operational definition of child sexual abuse as legislated by the Province of Alberta Child Welfare Act:

> A child is sexually abused if the child is inappropriately exposed or subjected to sexual contact, activity, or behavior.
>
> Section 1 (3) (c) p. 6.

Criteria for Sample Inclusion

Three criteria had to be satisfied in order for a child sexual abuse case to be included in the study. First, cases alleging child sexual abuse had to be referred to Alberta Social Services during the 1985 calendar year. The abuse itself did not have to occur in 1985, but must have been referred for investigation between January 1, 1985 and December 31, 1985.

The location to which the child sexual abuse was reported was the focus of the second criterion. To be included in this study the referral had to be made to the specified region mentioned above. The second criterion was met if the referral was actually investigated by a child welfare worker within the region under study.

The third criterion to be considered was assessment. To be included in the study, the investigating social worker was required to have assessed that child sexual abuse had indeed occurred.

The sample was therefore defined as all cases of alleged child sexual abuse referred to Alberta Social Services in 1985; investigated by a child welfare worker within the identified region; and in which the alleged sexual abuse was assessed as actually having occurred.

Sample

Having defined the sample via the above three criteria, the next step was to gather an inventory of all child welfare files. The study initially identified a preliminary group of 539 alleged victims who met the first two criteria. These 539 files were then reviewed to screen out those that did not meet the third criterion. This process rendered 191 cases in which the investigating social workers concluded that child sexual abuse had occurred. It is these 191 victims that form the final sample for this study.

Validity and Reliability

A data-gathering instrument was designed based upon a review of professional literature on child sexual abuse. Three employees of Alberta Social Services tested the instrument to affirm its content validity. Upon completion of this process additions, modifications, and deletions were made in format and operational definitions of the instrument to increase validity.

A test for interrater reliability rendered an error rate of less than one percent. Twenty percent of all files (109) included in this study were randomly checked for reliability of data collection. Seven errors were present in a total of 9,146 responses. Where there was error (disagreement between the principal data gatherer and the person checking reliability) the files were rechecked and corrections were made.

FINDINGS AND DISCUSSION

Four separate variables are highlighted in this article: victim, victim's family, perpetrator, and occurrence. Each variable will be delineated into related subvariables for presentation purposes.

Victim

Perhaps the largest body of literature concerning child sexual abuse is that which exists about the victim (e.g., Helfer, 1982). This study reports on five victim-related subvariables: gender, age, relationship to the perpetrator, number of perpetrators, and previous history as a victim. These five subvariables were chosen because of their prevalence in the literature.

The first of five subvariables concerning the victim was the child's gender. Mrazek, Lynch, and Bentovim (1983) have stated that there are significantly larger numbers of reported female child sexual abuse victims than male victims. Other authors indicate similar findings (Erickson, Walbek, & Seely, 1988; Pierce & Pierce, 1985b). Generally, the literature indicates that between 80 to 90 percent of all reported victims are female (e.g., Pierce & Pierce, 1985b). Our analysis of Canadian data is in agreement with the findings presented below. As can been seen from Table C-1, 84 percent of all reported victims of child sexual abuse were female.

Age of the victim at the onset of abuse was the second subvariable examined. Meddin (1985) reported that the younger child is viewed as being at greater risk of sexual abuse than the older child. An interesting

Table C-1   Victims of Child Sexual Abuse

Variables		Number	Percent
Gender:	Males	30	16%
	Females	161	84%
Mean Age of Child at Onset of Abuse:	Males	8.0	
	Females	8.4	
	Combined	8.3	
Relationship to the Perpetrator:			
Father Role (Biological)		49	27%
Father Role (Nonbiological)		49	27%
Mother Role (Biological)		3	2%
Female Sibling		2	1%
Male Sibling		17	9%
Uncle		12	6%
Male Cousin		7	4%
Grandfather		7	4%
Significant Other (Nonrelated)		38	21%
Missing Data		7	
Previous History as a Victim:			
Yes		38	26%
No		109	74%
Missing Data		44	
Number of Different Perpetrators:			
Single Perpetrator		179	94%
Multiple Perpetrators		11	6%
Missing Data		1	

relationship between gender and age of the child sexual abuse victim is indicated by many studies. For example, the age of a male victim at the time of reporting was significantly lower than for female victims (Russell, 1983). This study found that the mean age at onset of abuse for males and females was 8.3 years. Furthermore, this study's findings were congruent with the literature in which the mean age for males at the onset of abuse was 8 years compared to 8.4 years for females.

The third subvariable studied was the relationship of the victim to the perpetrator. Relationship to the perpetrator can be further broken down into two categories: intrafamilial or extrafamilial. For the purposes of this study, intrafamilial child sexual abuse occurred when there was a blood

Table C-2   Victims of Sexual Abuse
                       and Their Families

Variables	Number	Percent
Parental Structure:		
Two Parent	115	61%
Single Parent	71	38%
Extended Family	2	1%
Missing Data	3	
Other Known Family Victims:		
None	107	60%
One	44	25%
Two	26	14%
Three	2	1%
Missing Data	12	
Known Prior Sexual Abuse of Parents:		
Mother	29	58%
None	17	34%
Father	3	6%
Both	1	2%
Missing Data	141	

or legal familial relationship between the victim and the perpetrator. Extrafamilial child sexual abuse occurred when there was no blood or legal familial relationship between the victim and the perpetrator.

Summit (1980) reported that the vast majority of perpetrators came from the victim's family. This study also identified intrafamilial child sexual abuse as predominant. In 54 percent of all reported cases the perpetrator was the individual in the father role. In addition, once all intrafamilial relationships were accounted for, 79 percent of child sexual abuse victims were related either by blood or legal ties to the perpetrator. The remaining 21 percent of perpetrators were not related to the victims.

The child's previous history as a victim (i.e., physical abuse, sexual and emotional abuse, neglect) was the fourth subvariable examined. Pierce and Pierce (1985a) reported that over one-third of all substantiated cases of child sexual abuse had been previously reported as allegations of abuse other than sexual. Canadian data yield similar results (e.g., Corsini-Munt, 1982). In this study, a previous history of child abuse had been recorded for 26 percent of the 191 child sexual abuse victims.

Table C-3   Perpetrator Characteristics

Variables		Number	Percent
Gender:	Male	186	98%
	Female	4	2%
	Missing Data	1	
Mean Age of Perpetrator at Onset:	Male	27.5	
	Female	22.5	
	Combined	27.0	
Previous History of Abuse as a Victim:			
Yes		16	67%
No		8	33%
Missing Data		167	
Previous History of Abuse as a Perpetrator:			
Yes		91	100%
No		0	0%
Missing Data		100	
Relationship to the Victim:			
Father Role (Biological)		49	27%
Father Role (Nonbiological)		49	27%
Significant Other (Nonrelated)		38	21%
Male Sibling		17	9%
Uncle		12	5%
Male Cousin		7	4%
Grandfather		7	4%
Mother Role (Biological)		3	2%
Female Sibling		2	1%
Missing Data		7	

The final subvariable examined was the number of different perpetrators involved with the victim. Evidence indicates that victims with multiple perpetrators have greater difficulty in treatment after the occurrences than do those with a single perpetrator (e.g., Greenburg, 1983). This study reports that 94 percent of the victims had a single perpetrator, while six percent experienced multiple perpetrators. Data from the U.S. are similar in that only one perpetrator was involved in 90 percent of 304 child sexual abuse cases (Pierce & Pierce, 1985a).

Victim's Family

Many variables have been associated with the family of the child sexual abuse victim. This section examines three: parental structure, other known family victims, and known prior sexual abuse of parents (see Table C-2).

Parental structure was the first of three subvariables concerning the victim's family. Family constellation is important to every child, especially in terms of risk to the child's safety and development. There is a large body of literature concerning family structure in relation to child sexual abuse (Dietz & Craft, 1980). This study defined parental structure as the adult(s) responsible for the child victim. Possibilities of family structure include: one natural parent, both natural parents, one natural parent and another parent, or an extended family living arrangement.

Upon reviewing the literature, Mannarino and Cohen (1986) found that the majority of child sexual abuse victims were living with both parents at the time of the abuse. This study's findings were consistent with those of Mannarino and Cohen. Sixty-one percent of the victims of child sexual abuse were living in two-parent families at the time of abuse. In comparison, Pierce and Pierce (1985a) found that 25 percent of victims were living in homes headed by a single parent. Once again, this study was similar in its findings in that 38 percent of the victims were living in single-parent homes at the onset of abuse.

The Perpetrator

There are many issues to be considered when examining the perpetrator in child sexual abuse. This section considers five subvariables: the perpetrator's gender, mean age of the perpetrator at the onset of abusive behavior, previous history of abuse as a victim, previous history of abuse as a perpetrator, and relationship to the victim (see Table C-3).

The first subvariable concerning the perpetrator was gender. There is an abundance of literature indicating that males predominate in the commission of child sexual abuse (Finkelhor & Hotaling, 1984). This study's findings are clearly consistent with the literature in that 98 percent of the perpetrators were male.

The literature suggests (e.g., Pierce & Pierce, 1985a), that the mean age of the perpetrator was 34 years. This study's findings indicate that

Table C-4   Victims and Situational Variables

Variables	Number	Percent
Primary Sexual Act:		
Fondling of Genitalia	79	46%
Vaginal Penetration	40	24%
Attempted Vaginal Penetration	12	7%
Exposure	9	5%
Anal Penetration	8	5%
Fellatio	5	3%
Cunnilingus	3	2%
Kissing	2	1%
Not Classified	8	5%
Missing Data	21	
Mean Duration of Abuse		
(in months): Male	15.0	
Female	21.7	
Combined	21.1	
Frequency:		
Multiple Occurrences	126	79%
Single Occurrence	34	21%
Missing Data	31	

the mean age of the perpetrator (male and female combined) at the onset of abuse to be 27.0 years—seven years younger than the U.S. data.

One of the prime issues regarding sexual offenders is their relationship to the victim. Many studies in the literature point out that the vast majority of perpetrators are from within the child's family (Summit, 1980). This study found that 79 percent of all perpetrators were in fact from within the child's family. These perpetrators were usually men in the father role. Only 21 percent of the perpetrators were individuals outside of the family, or in other words, of no relation to the victim.

The Occurrence

The fourth variable that plays an important role in the study of child sexual abuse is the occurrence itself. Three subvariables related to the occurrence were considered: the primary sexual act, duration of the abuse, and the frequency of occurrence (see Table C-4).

The first subvariable regarding the occurrence is the primary sexual act. Attitudes toward child sexual abuse are documented to be influenced by the abusive activities that occur (Wilk & McCarthy, 1986). For example, as people in authority, social workers tend to be more tolerant of one incident of fondling than they are of multiple events of sexual intercourse (Finkelhor, 1983). Also related to the type of activity is the question of upon whom the sexual act was performed. The victim may be coerced into performing a sexual act on the perpetrator just as frequently as the perpetrator victimizes the child.

Berliner and Conte (1981) reported that 64 percent of the time the primary abusive act was fondling of genitalia. This study also reports that fondling was the sexual act that occurred most frequently. Furthermore, Baumann, Kasper and Alford (1984) found that penetration occurred in less than one-third of child sexual abuse cases. This analysis found that vaginal penetration took place in 23 percent of the child sexual abuse cases—approximately 10 percentage points less than the U.S. data.

The second subvariable to be considered in regard to occurrence is the duration of abuse. Studies indicate that large numbers of child sexual abuse situations continue for years prior to the victim's disclosure to a person in authority. Again this study was congruent with the literature. The mean duration of abuse for males and females combined was 21.1 months.

Frequency of occurrence in child sexual abuse has been given due attention in the literature (Finkelhor, 1983). The difference between a single occurrence and multiple occurrences is an important consideration in victim treatment and perpetrator disposition. Berliner and Conte (1981) have reported that the majority of cases (66%) include multiple occurrences. In contrast, they found that only 17 percent of the cases consisted of a single incident of abuse. This study was consistent with the above data. Multiple occurrences were present in 79 percent of the cases, as opposed to 21 percent reporting single occurrences.

IMPLICATIONS

Monitoring the profiles of the victim, the family, and the perpetrator have great implications for human service professionals concerned with child sexual abuse. Community education can be focused to the population with the greatest need. Armed with characteristic data, child care workers may be able to identify the victim, thereby preventing further abuse.

In constructing the four tables presented in this study, the authors found a great deal of missing data. Missing information for any one variable ranged as high as 87 percent. This has implications for the development of a standardized data collection format to be used in child sexual abuse investigations.

The similarity of Canadian data to that from the United States has implications for further service development. The United States has a proliferation of information concerning child sexual abuse. Treatment programs, policymakers, and child care workers could benefit greatly from the experience and expertise developed in the southern half of this continent. However, further study is necessary to validate and track the apparent current similarities.

SUMMARY

In summary, this research note has presented Canadian-based data on the victims of child sexual abuse. The information was compiled from the files of one Alberta Social Service region. Specific variables described were: characteristics of the victim, the victim's family structure, a profile of the perpetrator, as well as details pertaining to the sexually abusive occurrence.

At the risk of overgeneralizing, this study found that a majority of the victims of child sexual abuse were females whose average age was 8.4 years, with single perpetrators who were their fathers. In addition, a majority of the victims did not have previous histories of sexual abuse. They came from two-parent families and there were no other known family victims. The perpetrators were males whose average age was 27.5 years old. The primary sexual act included multiple occurrences of the fondling of genitalia.

REFERENCES

Alberta Social Services. (1984). *Province of Alberta Child Welfare Act.* Edmonton, AB: Author.

Baumann, R.C., Kasper, J.C., & Alford, J.M. (1984). The child sex abusers. *Corrective and Social Psychiatry, 29-30,* 76-81.

Berliner, L., & Conte, J.R. (1981). Sexual abuse of children: Implications for practice. *Social Casework, 62,* 601-606.

Butler, S. (1978). *Conspiracy of silence.* San Francisco, CA: New Glide Publications.

Corsini-Munt, L.A. (1982). A Canadian study: Sexual abuse of children and adolescents. In B. Schlesinger (Ed.), *Sexual abuse of children: A resource guide and annotated bibliography.* Toronto, ON: University of Toronto Press.

Dietz, C.A., & Craft, J.L. (1980). Family dynamics of incest: A new perspective. *Social Casework, 61,* 602-609.

Erickson, W.D., Walbek, N.H., & Seely, R.K. (1988). Behavior patterns of child molesters. *Archives of Sexual Behavior, 7,* 77-86.

Faria, G., & Belohlavek, N. (1984). Treating female adult survivors of childhood incest. *Social Casework, 65,* 465-477.

Finkelhor, D. (1983). Removing the child—prosecuting the offender in cases of sexual abuse: Evidence from the National Reporting System for Child Abuse and Neglect. *Child Abuse and Neglect, 7,* 195-205.

Finkelhor, D., & Hotaling, G.T. (1984). Sexual abuse in the national incidence study of child abuse and neglect: An appraisal. *Child Abuse and Neglect, 8,* 23-33.

Giaretto, H. (1976). Humanistic treatment of father daughter incest. In R.E. Helfer & C.H. Kempe (Eds.), *Child abuse and neglect: The family and the community* (pp. 120-144). Cambridge, MA: Ballinger.

Giaretto, H. (1982). *Integrated treatment of child sexual abuse: A treatment manual.* Berkeley, CA: Science and Behavior Books.

Greenburg, N. (1983). Remarks to the national medical center's conference on sexual abuse. In D. Finkelhor, Removing the child—prosecuting the offender in cases of sexual abuse: Evidence from the national reporting system for child abuse and neglect. *Child Abuse and Neglect, 7,* 195-205.

Helfer, R.E. (1982). A review of the literature on the prevention of child abuse and neglect. *Child Abuse and Neglect, 6,* 251-266.

Howes, C. (May 25, 1986). Incest: Dark secrets confronted. *Calgary Herald,* 1.

Justice, B., & Justice, R. (1979). *The broken taboo: Sex in the family.* New York: Human Sciences Press.

Mannarino, A.P., & Cohen, J.A. (1986). A clinical-demographic study of sexually abused children. *Child Abuse and Neglect, 10,* 17-23.

Meddin, B.J. (1985). The assessment risk in child abuse and neglect case investigations. *Child Abuse and Neglect, 9,* 57-62.

Mrazek, P.J., Lynch, M.A., & Bentovim, A. (1983). Sexual abuse of children in the United Kingdom. *Child Abuse and Neglect, 7,* 147-153.

Pierce, R.L., & Pierce, L.H. (1985a). Analysis of sexual abuse hotline reports. *Child Abuse and Neglect, 9,* 37-45.

Pierce, R.L., & Pierce, L.H. (1985b). The sexually abused child: A comparison of male and female victims. *Child Abuse and Neglect, 9,* 191-199.

Russell, A.B., & Trainor, C.M. (1984). *Trends in child abuse and neglect: A national perspective.* Denver, CO: American Humane Association.

Russell, D.E. (1983). The incidence and prevalence of intrafamilial and extrafamilial sexual abuse of female children. *Child Abuse and Neglect, 7,* 133-146.

Sgroi, S.M. (Ed.). (1982). *Handbook of clinical intervention in child sexual abuse.* Toronto, ON: Lexington Books.

Summit, R. (1980). *Typical characteristics of father-daughter incest: A guide for investigation.* Unpublished paper. Los Angeles, CA: Harbor UCLA Medical Center.

Wilk, R.J., & McCarthy C.R. (1986). Intervention in child sexual abuse: A survey of attitudes. *Social Casework, 67,* 20-26.

Wyatt, G.E., & Peters, S.D. (1986). Issues in the definition of child sexual abuse in prevalence research. *Child Abuse and Neglect, 10,* 231-240.

Donna M. Phillips
Joseph P. Hornick

S t u d y   D

An Evaluation of a Psychological Treatment Component

EW STUDIES of homeless male alcoholics include a systematic assessment of their personalities. One such study (Blumberg, Shipley, & Shandler, 1973) found the group had a high degree of social pathology, which would be a severe hindrance to their being accepted as members of a larger community. They also found the men were depressed, and experienced much dissatisfaction with themselves.

Holloway (1970) found the homeless male alcoholic to have an inability to cope with small problems and minor inconveniences, resentment and hatred toward parents, and a longing for affection and sympathy. In summary, this population appears to be psychologically unhealthy, especially in terms of depression and sociopathy.

These studies measured the psychological health of homeless alcoholic men in general. There is an even greater lack of literature that considers the impact of treatment programs on this population's psychological health. It must be emphasized that this research example is only presenting the results of the psychological component (one of three) of the treatment program for a community house for homeless alcoholic men.

PURPOSE OF STUDY

A comprehensive study was initially conducted to test the effectiveness of several aspects of a community house for homeless alcoholic men. Program objectives included improving residents' physical, psychological, and social functioning. These three program components were each evaluated using three separate instruments.

The purpose of this sample evaluation study is to briefly report the findings related to only the program's psychological health component. As existing literature in the area indicates homeless alcoholic men are psychologically less healthy than the general population, it is predicted that residents' psychological health will improve over the course of their stay in the community house.

PROGRAM DESCRIPTION

The community house evaluated in this study is a long-term residence designed to help homeless destitute men. However, as more than 90% of its residents have self-identified alcohol problems, the program has been tailored to meet the needs of homeless alcoholic men. (To protect the anonymity of the agency under evaluation, it will be referred to as the "House.")

The program is based on the premise that, by offering the men a place to live where they are treated with respect and are given support, responsibility, and access to available resources, they will have the opportunity to become responsible and contributing members of society.

The program under evaluation is run by a private, voluntary, nonprofit organization. The services are provided to homeless men of any religion, race, or background. Although most of the residents have chronic drug and/or alcohol problems, this is not a requirement of admission to the program.

The House consists of two adjacent residences with accommodations for 20 men. It has consistently operated at full capacity. The House has four paid staff: a director, and one evening, one night, and one weekend supervisor. The staff perform a number of duties, including: (a) designing and implementing plans for each resident's rehabilitation, (b) giving attention to residents' physical health problems, (c) supervising residents' work programs, (d) arranging social activities, (e) providing informal counseling, (f) arranging referrals to outside agencies, (g) maintaining

---

Goals:

(1)   To help the residents achieve personal fulfilment.
(2)   To help the residents become responsible, contributing members of society.

Objectives: **Activities:**

1.0   To improve   -   provide supportive,
         psychological func-   homelike atmosphere
         tioning.   with minimal rules
1.1   To decrease   -   refer to outside
         depression anxiety,   agencies, groups for
         guilt, resentment,   counseling
         suspiciousness,   -   provide information,
         psychological   counseling, and the
         inadequacy, and inse-   opportunity for
         curity.   mutual support

Figure D-1   Program Goals, Psychological Health
                      Objectives, and Activities

records, and (h) enforcing house rules. These duties are performed in an environment where a minimum number of rules are in existence. The residents are expected to be responsible for, and deal with, the consequences of their actions.

Figure D-1 on the following page outlines the House's general goals and specific psychological health objectives. The column on the right delineates the activities performed by program staff as they attempt to meet these objectives.

METHODOLOGY

This section presents the study's research design, sample, and the measuring instrument that was used to measure the dependent variable.

Research Design

A one-group pretest-posttest design was used to test the participants' movement toward improved psychological health. A standardized measuring instrument was self-administered once ($N = 22$), then again six weeks later ($N = 9$) to evaluate pretest-posttest differences.

Additional analyses compared the psychological profiles of program successes and program failures. Nine participants were characterized as program successes and the remaining thirteen were identified as program failures. An unplanned discharge, characterized by a return to drinking, was identified as a type of program failure. The assignment of participants to "success" and "failure" groups enabled a comparative analysis between those who stayed sober and in the program for an extended period of time (at least 3 months), and those who were unable to stay sober and "dropped out" of the program. This 3-month period of time was chosen as an indicator of program success based on previous research (Katz, 1986; Orford & Hawker, 1974; Rubington, 1970).

Sample and Measuring Instrument

All residents were asked to participate, and all who agreed did so voluntarily. The response rate to the pretesting was consistently 80 percent.

Due to admission criteria of the program, no participants were under 18 years of age, female, or showing signs of severe mental illness or mental incompetence. They had to be capable of climbing stairs. Thus, no severely physically disabled participants took part. Most participants had no other place to live when they requested admission to the House. A few were not destitute in this sense, but they stated they needed a sober environment. The two primary problems identified on the participants' admission were homelessness and alcoholism.

The high rate of sample attrition posed a problem, which is typical in studies of homeless, transient men. Of the 22 participants interviewed, 9 remained at the House for over 6 weeks and thus could be posttested.

Data were collected by the use of a standardized measuring instrument—the Clinical Analysis Questionnaire (CAQ) (Krug & Cattel, 1980). The CAQ questionnaire consists of 272 multiple choice questions which respondents answer about themselves. The CAQ is an instrument that simultaneously measures normal and pathological trait levels and

Normal Personality Traits	Clinical Factors	Second-Order Factors
A: Warmth	D1: Hypochondriasis	Ex: Extroversion
B: Intelligence	D2: Suicidal depression	Ax: Anxiety
C: Emotional stability	D3: Agitation	Ct: Tough poise
E: Dominance	D4: Anxious depression	In: Independence
F: Impulsivity	D5: Low energy level	Se: Superego
G: Conformity	D6: Guilt & resentment	So: Socialization
H: Boldness	D7: Boredom & withdrawal	D: Depression
I: Sensitivity	Pa: Paranoia	P: Psychoticism
L: Suspiciousness	Pp: Psychopathic deviation	Ne: Neuroticism
M: Imagination	Sc: Schizophrenia	
N: Shrewdness		
O: Insecurity		
Q2: Self-sufficiency		
Q4: Tension		
Q3: Self-discipline		

Figure D-2   The CAQ Scales

provides a multidimensional profile of the individual. It consists of 28 scales: 16 measure normal personality traits; 7 measure primary manifestations of depression; and 5 measure traits from the MMPI pool. In addition to the 28 primary scales, it is possible to calculate second-order scores. By combining the primary scale scores in certain ways, these second-order scores indicate patterns such as Extroversion, Anxiety, Neuroticism, etc. Figure D-2 outlines the 37 CAQ scales.

FINDINGS AND DISCUSSION

This section presents the study's findings in two broad areas: (1) the comparison of pretest and posttest data, and (2) a comparison of program successes and failures.

Comparison of Pretest and Posttest Data

Due to sample attrition the sample size in the pretest-posttest data, analysis was greatly reduced from 22 to nine participants. A six-week treatment period was established, although all participants were in the program for a longer period of time. Results indicate that the group of nine participants progressed in terms of their psychological functioning.

Table D-1 shows that participants' mean posttest scores differ notably from their mean pretest scores on 10 of the 37 CAQ scales. These differences indicate that, at time two, participants were somewhat more dependent (I+, M+), bored (D7+), and tended to be more realistic (Sc-), less sociopathic (Se+), and less depressed (D-) than at time one. They also suggest participants were more mindful of rules (N+, Q3+), although they tended to avoid people more (D3-), and that they were better able to keep their emotions in order (N+, Q3+) and were less apt to have negative feelings of self-worth (Ps-) (Krug & Cattel, 1980).

These changes indicate that the program was successful in decreasing participants' levels of deviance, and in increasing their levels of self-worth. In doing so, the program tended to constrain their independence, which is not unusual in any semi-instructional program. This may have been the only way to positively affect the sociopathy but, once dependent on the program, participants become bored and restless.

Regardless of changes made during the six-week period of the evaluation study, participants' overall psychological profiles remained abnormal, showing high levels of suicidal disgust, anxious depression, guilt and resentment, paranoia, schizophrenia, and general psychosis. This group of men showed a need for mental health assessment and treatment, as is consistent with previous studies (Blumberg, Shipley, & Shandler, 1973; Holloway, 1970).

Comparison of Program Successes and Failures

Participants were assigned to a "success" group or a "failure" group. Assignment to these groups was based on whether the participant stayed in the program or dropped out, as is described in the methodology section of this report.

No statistically significant differences were found between the successes and failures on the CAQ, although clinically relevant differences were evident on five of the CAQ personality scales (i.e., the

Table D-1   Participants' Mean Pretest and Posttest
                     CAQ Scores

CAQ Factors	Pretest	Posttest	Difference	t	p[1]
Normal sensitivity (I)	5.9	6.7	-.78	1.6	.06
Imagination (M)	5.1	6.3	-1.22	2.2	.03
Shrewdness (N)	6.4	7.4	-1.00	2.0	.04
Self-discipline (Q3)	3.4	4.4	-1.00	1.6	.07
Clinical agitation (D3)	3.7	2.8	.89	1.8	.05
Boredom & withdrawal (D7)	5.6	6.1	-.56	1.2	.12
Schizophrenia (Sc)	9.2	8.8	.44	1.8	.05
Psychological inadequacy (Ps)	8.2	7.4	.78	1.5	.07
Superego strength (Se)	3.7	4.5	-.58	1.4	.09
Depression (D)	7.3	6.7	.59	1.2	.10

[1] One-tailed test

suspiciousness, insecurity, tension, quilt and resentment, and anxiety scales). These differing scores on the CAQ scales indicate that the failures were more suspicious, insecure, tense, resentful, and anxious than the successes (Krug & Cattell, 1980). These differing personality traits could explain why a failure (a program dropout) may be more suspecting and less tolerant of a program such as this one, especially in view of his inability to accept criticism.

LIMITATIONS

A major weakness limiting the methodology of this study is the lack of a control or a comparison group. The transient nature of the homeless alcoholic population prevented the formation of a control group, and the lack of a similar program in the Calgary area prevented the formation of a comparison group.

The small sample size ($N = 9$) was a major study limitation. This resulted from both the small program size (the House has room for 20 men) and sample attrition. Further, having a small sample size made it difficult to achieve statistical significance in data analyses.

Forming aggregate CAQ profiles from individual cases resulted in regression toward the mean, causing a minimization of variation. This increased the need to carefully observe and report major trends that were not statistically significant.

Ideally, baseline data should have been collected on all the participants upon their admission to the program, and measurement should have been repeated at six-week intervals throughout their stay. This was not possible due to time limitations.

Participants were the only data source in the study. This has a weakening effect on the methodology, which should be supported by another source such as assessment by a psychologist (Blumburg, Shipley, & Shandler, 1973).

In summary, the major methodological limitations were: lack of a control or comparison group, small sample size, lack of baseline data collected on participants' admission to the program, and data being collected from a single source. These limitations should be considered while viewing the study's results and conclusions.

SUMMARY AND RECOMMENDATIONS

The purpose of this evaluation study was to test the effectiveness of a psychological heath component of a community residence for homeless alcoholic men. The program consisted of a homelike residence supervised by four staff members who provided day and night assistance and informal counseling.

The participants who remained in the program longer than three months and graduated from it ($N = 9$) showed a prolonged improvement in major aspects of their psychological functioning, although their overall level of functioning remained poor. The other client group, the dropouts, could not be posttested. However, Clinical Analysis Questionnaire results showed the dropouts to be more suspicious, insecure, resentful, and generally less tolerant of structured programs than the graduates.

The findings and conclusions of this study have led to a number of recommendations. These recommendations have relevance to both program development and evaluation research in this area. The four recommendations relevant to program development for homeless alcoholic men are:

1. The mental health assessment procedure of applicants to the program should be more rigorous and more clearly defined. This would enable proper screening and referral of those men in need of specific mental health counseling.

2. Program residents should be regularly referred for counseling.
3. Planned activities should be made available for residents, in order to avoid boredom and withdrawal.
4. Future development should include a final program phase that offers a more autonomous living situation for program graduates who may be somewhat dependent on the program.

In terms of the recommendations for future research in this area, further use of the Clinical Analysis Questionnaire to measure the psychological functioning of homeless alcoholic men should be encouraged. In addition, further evaluation research on programs for homeless alcoholic men is needed, especially research that utilizes control groups and multiple data sources. Lastly, follow-up studies of programs are recommended, to further explore the long-term effects of treatment on homeless alcoholic men.

REFERENCES

Bahr, H. (1969). Lifetime affiliation patterns of elderly and late-onset heavy drinkers on skid row. *Quarterly Journal of Studies on Alcohol, 30*, 645-656.

Bahr, H. (1973). *Skid Row: An introduction to disaffiliation*. New York: Oxford University Press.

Blumberg, L., Shipley, T., & Shandler, I. (1973). *Skid Row and its alternatives*. Philadelphia, PA: Temple University Press.

Cook, T. (1975). *Vagrant alcoholics*. London, England: Routledge & Kegan Paul.

Holloway, J. (1970). *They can't fit in*. London, England: Blackfriars Press.

Katz, L. (1966). The Salvation Army men's social service center results. *Studies on Alcohol, 27*, 636-647.

Krug, S.E., & Cattell, R.B. (1980). *Clinical analysis questionnaire manual*. Champaign, IL: Institute for Personality and Ability Testing.

Orford, J., & Hawker, A. (1974). An investigation of an alcoholism rehabilitation halfway house: The complex question of client motivation. *British Journal of Addictions, 69*, 315-323.

Rubington, E. (1970). Referral, past treatment contacts, and length of stay in a halfway house. *Quarterly Journal of Studies on Alcohol, 31*, 659-668.

Craig W. LeCroy
Cynthia C. Goodwin

S t u d y   E

New Directions in Teaching Social Work Methods: A Content Analysis of Course Outlines

SOCIAL WORK EDUCATION has undergone considerable change in the last two decades. As Constable (1984, p. 366) states "in the mid-1960s it became evident that developments in knowledge and in practice were outrunning the possibility of a single prescribed curriculum for the MSW degree." However, new curriculum issues surfaced with the greater acceptance of diversity within social work programs.

Social work educators began to debate each other. One such dispute involved the generic versus specific focus of social work education (Leighninger, 1980). Another debate looked at the extent to which a common foundation of practice exists (Aigner, 1984; Hartman, 1983).

Several attempts have been made to interpret and understand the nature of curriculum changes in social work education. For example, several articles have analyzed the Curriculum Policy Statement, compared it with its predecessor, and put it into the context of present-day social work education (Constable, 1984; Aigner, 1984; Hokenstad, 1984). Some educators examined the issues arising from these changes from a historical perspective, by seeing how changes took place and interpreting their significance (Constable, 1984). One study designed a questionnaire to examine ways in which generic content was being taught in graduate social work curricula (Bakalinsky, 1982).

Although various methods have added to our understanding of social work education, there is very little current information on course content in graduate schools of social work. Guzzetta (1982) conducted a content analysis of MSW programs, and found little change in overall program design. Yet, no information is available on the topics covered or the focus of instruction in practice courses. No scholar has been able to interpret this information in light of new CSWE policy and the changes occurring in the profession. That void prompted the present research, which uses course outlines to examine the content of graduate-level direct practice courses.

METHODOLOGY

The sources of data used in the study were the outlines for foundation practice courses currently being used by faculty who teach social work methods. The 93 schools of social work represented in the CSWE list of accredited graduate programs were conducted by telephone. Of all the schools conducted, 80 (87%) agreed to participate. Of the 93 schools contacted, 65 percent are represented in the final sample (i.e., submitted course outlines). In terms of the geographical distribution of the sample, 21 percent of the schools are in the West, 25 percent are in the East, 27 percent are in the Midwest, and 27 percent are in the South.

Each school was asked to provide the names of faculty members teaching a first-year direct practice or methods course. The 354 faculty members were requested to send a copy of their current course outline. A follow-up letter was sent to nonrespondents eight weeks after the initial mailing. A total of 188 course outlines was received. About 10 percent of the outlines were not usable because the outline was for an elective course rather than a required direct practice course. Some of the same outlines were submitted by more than one instructor, hence the actual number of course outlines does not match the number of course instructors.

The final response rate, which was based on the number of faculty identified and the number of course outlines received, was 58 percent, typical for this type of study (See Bakalinsky, 1982; Lauderdale, Grinnell, & McMurtry, 1980). The complexity of the sampling method makes it difficult to validate the accuracy of the data. However, over half of the schools that have MSW programs are represented and the response rate of the instructors meets expectations.

RESULTS

The following data were taken from the course outlines: topics covered in the course units, required readings, course assignments, and course textbooks. All of the data were subjected to an interrater reliability evaluation. The entire sample of course outlines was used in the reliability analysis. Each variable was categorized by two research assistants. Definitions were used for each variable to train the raters and enhance consistency in ratings. The authors used Cohen's kappa to calculate interrater reliability. It is a more conservative and reliable estimate than percent agreement because it controls for chance agreement.

The results of the reliability analysis are presented in Table E-1. In general, all of the data, except treatment process under course units, show adequate reliability.

Course Units

Each course outline was examined to determine the content covered throughout the class. Courses would typically be divided into sections labeled "the client-worker relationship" or "data collection." These course units were grouped into 10 categories. The number of units used in each course outline is presented in Table E-2 (percentages are based on total number of course outlines in the sample, $N = 170$).

The most frequently covered unit was Treatment Process (72%). This is not surprising: Social work methods courses should cover basic treatment issues such as contracting and goal setting. In addition, most courses dealt with introductory materials, the social work relationship, and assessment. Few of the courses covered crisis intervention, and only 19 percent presented material on research and practice evaluation. The recent emphasis on practice evaluation by CSWE (1982) makes the latter finding particularly striking. The new Curriculum Policy Statement directs schools to prepare students to "evaluate their own practice and contribute to the generation on knowledge for practice" (Council on Social Work Education, 1982, p. 8). Perhaps social work programs

Table E-1   Interrater Reliability of Course
                        Outline Variables (Cohen's Kappa)

Course Units		Course Texts	
Introduction	.95	Compton & Galaway	.100
Social Work Relationship	.92	Hepworth & Larsen	.97
Ethnic-sensitive Practice	.87	Germain & Gitterman	.100
Data Collection	.72	Green	NA
Assessment	.75	Pincus & Minahan	NA
Crisis Intervention	NA	Garvin & Seabury	NA
Treatment Process	.52	Shulman	NA
Research/Evaluation	.79		
Termination	.83		

Secondary Texts		**Assignments**	
Hollis & Woods	.83	Assessment	.73
Ruperstein & Block	.85	Final exam	.96
Germain & Gitterman	.92	Midterm exam	.98
Pincus & Minahan	NA	Term Paper	.86
Egan	NA	Written Assignment	.63
Compton & Galaway	NA	Interview	.78
		Log	NA
		Experience	NA

Required Reading[a]	
Research articles	.76
Minority articles	.82

[a]Interrater reliability based on Pearson's Correlation Coefficient.
NA = not applicable, frequency of occurrence not large enough.

currently use research courses to meet this objective. Nonetheless, the best forum still is undetermined. Without clear guidelines, practice evaluation may receive inadequate coverage. Worse yet, it may not be taught at all.

Very few courses read published research. A count of the authors determined the number of research articles listed as required reading. Required reading was defined as any material listed in the course outlines that the instructor clearly expected the students to read. These articles had to include the use of systematic observation and standardized procedures to be considered research. Our results revealed a mean of only .67—less than one article per course. Few courses used research

Table E-2   Course Units Used in the
                     Direct Practice Courses

Textbooks	Percent of Sample	Number of Occurrences
Introduction	70.6	120
Social Work Relationship	61.8	105
Ethnic-sensitive Practice	30.6	52
Data Collection	46.5	79
Assessment	68.2	116
Crisis Intervention	5.9	10
Treatment Process	71.8	122
Research/Practice Evaluation	17.6	30
Termination	54.1	92

Note: The textbooks listed in this table are cited
         as references.

articles in addition to the required textbooks. Although CSWE states that recent research be taught in practice courses (Council on Social Work Education, 1982, p. 8), evidence suggests that only small numbers of empirical studies are actually incorporated into syllabi.

The CSWE guidelines are quite clear: "Both the professional foundation and the advanced concentration curricula must give explicit attention to the patterns and consequences of discrimination and oppression, providing both theoretical and practice content about groups that continue to be subjected to oppression and those that are emerging into new social roles with greater freedom and visibility" (Council on Social Work Education, 1982, p. 6). Analyses of course outlines indicate

Table E-3   Required Textbooks
                     Used in Courses

Textbooks	Percent of Sample	Number of Times Used
Compton & Galaway	17.1	29
Hepworth & Larsen	12.9	22
Germain & Gitterman	4.1	7
Green	2.9	5
Pincus & Minahan	3.5	6
Garvin & Seabury	3.5	6
Shulman	2.4	4

Note: The textbooks listed in this table
         are cited as references.

that only 31 percent of practice courses devoted much attention to ethnic sensitivity issues. This appears to be a serious omission: Professional social work practice necessitates study of these issues.

Required Reading

We compiled a list of the textbooks and readings most frequently used in practice courses. It was an effort to better understand the nature of those courses; textbook choice reveals much about the instructor's methods and assumptions.

Analysis of the list of required readings indicates that ethnicity issues (i.e., theoretical approaches to ethnicity, unrelated to particular ethnic groups) were completely absent from 42 percent of the course outlines. Another 22 percent of the course outlines included one or two articles on a minority group. Less than a quarter of the course outlines included a unit on minorities. These results suggest a need to reexamine the status of minority content in the curriculum.

Table E-3 lists the primary textbook for the class. Only one textbook was considered "primary"; if two or more textbooks were used, then the textbook with the larger amount of required reading was designated the primary textbook. Since many courses used more than one textbook Table E-4 lists other required textbooks, designated "secondary textbooks." Both tables show the number of times each textbook was used, according to the course outlines.

Table E-3 shows that the two most frequently used textbooks are the Compton and Galaway and the Hepworth and Larsen. Both books cover many of the course units reviewed earlier, such as: knowledge and values in social work, the social worker/client relationship, and the treatment process. However, the two texts differ in the presentation of the material. The Hepworth and Larsen text is competency-based and skills-oriented; the Compton and Galaway book follows a generic format. For example, in Compton and Galaway, treatment process is presented in a problem-solving format: The authors offer a conceptual framework rather than a guide to action.

In contrast, Hepworth and Larsen describe treatment process in an action- oriented set of guidelines for practice. In the past, social work methods classes frequently used the Pincus and Minahan textbook. Its popularity dropped sharply: At the time of this study, only 3.5 percent

Table E-4   Secondary Textbooks Used in Courses

Textbooks	Percent of Sample	Number of Times Used
Hollis & Woods	8.2	14
Ruperstein & Block	4.7	8
Germain & Gitterman	4.7	8
Pincus & Minahan	3.5	6
Egan	2.9	5
Compton & Galaway	2.9	5

Note: The textbooks listed in this table are cited as references.

of practice courses used it as primary text. The text lacks clear practice guidelines; this may account for its recent disfavor. Compton and Galaway replaced Pincus and Minahan as the most popular textbook because the former is more easily translated into those guidelines. Thus, it appears that action-oriented and task-centered methods are increasingly being used to teach social work practice. The newer models of education probably are the result of increased emphasis on social work practice outcomes. However, these speculations clearly are open to many interpretations.

Table E-5   Most Frequently Given Assignments

Assignments	Percent of Sample	Number of Times Assignment Appeared In Sample
Assessment Evaluation	22.4	38
Final Exam	21.2	36
Midterm Exam	20.0	34
Term Paper	15.9	27
Written Assignment	15.3	26
Analysis of an Interview	11.8	20
Log of a Placement	3.5	6
Personal Experience	2.9	5

Assignments

We also derived data on the types of grading criteria from the course outlines. Table E-5 presents these results. The most frequent assignments were assessments and psychosocial evaluations. Most of the assignments represent typical course requirements: exams, finals, term papers, and written assignments. Two assignments were assigned infrequently: analysis of an interview (11.8% of courses) and journal of placement experiences (3.5% of courses). It is hard to determine if this differs from previous practices.

Skills Training

In order to assess the extent to which courses included skills instruction a short questionnaire was attached to the course outline request. Some instructors returned course outlines but failed to return the questionnaire; they received follow-up letters and phone calls. Almost all (92%) of the instructors included in the study completed the additional questionnaire. A majority of the courses (70%) included some type of skills instruction. A few (12%) had none. Along with more of a competency-based curriculum, it appears practice courses incorporate more skills content than ever before. Historically, it was assumed that students would learn the necessary skills in the field. Schools of social work now try to ensure that practice skills are learned in the classroom and refined in the field.

DISCUSSION

Various attempts have been made to understand current directions in social work. Those attempts never examined the way social work practice is taught in schools of social work across the country.

This analysis suggests some interesting patterns in the teaching of social work and raises some important questions. For example, how consistent are MSW courses in schools of social work across the country? This study found reasonable consistency in basic educational content. In particular, most courses included units on the social worker/client relationship, assessment, treatment process, and termination. Many courses used similar reading for these units. Classic articles such as Seabury's (1976) article, "The Contract: Uses, Abuses and Limitations" Kadushin's (1963) article "Diagnosis and Evaluation for Almost all Occasions," and Germain and Gitterman's (1976) "Social Work Practice: A Life Model" were used in most of course readings. A large number of the required readings come from professional journals.

In a review of CSWE policy changes, Constable (1984, p. 367) notes that programmatic "differences, together with more obvious differences in the way programs identify themselves and conceive of their purpose, suggest that MSW programs are becoming less comparable over time." However, the data from this study suggest that the basic methods of social work education are comparable, at least in the first year. The advanced curriculum may be less comparable, but the initial year of direct practice appears to be fairly uniform. This leads to a further question. How comparable should we expect social work courses to be? This question (like many others) about social work education needs further study.

While there may be some common features across curricula there are clearly omissions in curriculum content. The most glaring omission is that only 30.6 percent of the course outlines included a unit on ethnic practice. In addition, the analysis of required readings found that general minority content was absent in 42 percent of the course outlines. These two findings suggest that many courses do not include anything directly relevant to ethnic practice. Ethnic content perhaps is covered in discussion and lecture. Alternatively, this "missing" content may be included in other courses. In addition, the CSWE call for increased emphasis on minority content may have resulted in the assimilation of these issues into every course unit. Nonetheless, 42 percent of courses had no readings on ethnic-sensitive practice. Students should read about minority issues relevant to the practice of social work. The CSWE requirement for increased minority content may ultimately contribute to a lack of minority content. Further research should examine this issue.

This omission calls into question the willingness of schools to conform to CSWE curriculum policy. The low percentages of research and practice evaluations also form such doubts.

Although there is a degree of uniformity in the social work curriculum, the profession lacks standardized course content. If, as Constable and others argue, social workers are becoming less comparable with each other, then perhaps CSWE should support efforts toward producing greater conformity in the foundation year.

Table E-6	Suggested Curriculum for Social Work Practice

1. Purpose and Objectives of Social Work Practice
2. Conceptual Frameworks for Social Work Practice
3. Knowledge and Values for Social Work Practice
4. The Social Work Relationship
5. Data Collection and Initial Contacts
6. Social Work Interviewing
7. Social Work with Special Populations
8. Assessment and Diagnosis
9. Contracting and Goal Setting
10. Treatment Strategies
11. Practice Evaluation
12. Termination

The authors propose that the course units identified in Table E-6 be included in all foundation year practice courses. This table represents the curriculum units frequently used in social work classes for direct practice. If the profession wants to increase uniformity across social work schools, a more standard curriculum is needed to enhance this consistency. Table E-6 serves as a preliminary guide. A more detailed set of recommendations could be provided to schools of social work. These recommendations might describe common objectives for suggested course units. However, increased consistency of educational objectives through uniform procedures is likely to be controversial.

There are several limitations to this study. The sampling frame consisted of only 58 percent of the population. The reliability of the sample is open to question; the sample itself must be interpreted in a circumspect fashion. It should also be noted that the meaning of the data is based on the authors' interpretation. For example, the idea that action-oriented task centered approaches are replacing the conceptual approaches is based solely on analysis of required textbooks for the courses. Furthermore, changes of this nature cannot be established in cross-sectional research study.

This study rests on the assumption that course syllabi reflect what is actually taught. Course outlines give one type of picture. In many ways it is an incomplete picture of what actually happens in a course. A course outline does not record the lectures, exercises and class discussions. In addition, the authors' categorizations may not accurately reflect content. For example, practice evaluation appeared to be omitted from most of the courses. However, practice evaluation may be covered under different course units, such as intervention procedures or termination. Nevertheless, course outlines are highly revealing documents. They are important symbols of educational values of social work. They also carry suggestions for the improvement of social work education.

REFERENCES

Aigner, S.M. (1984). The curriculum policy: Implications of an emergent consensus. *Journal of Education for Social Work, 20,* 5-14.

Bakalinsky, R. (1982). Generic practice in graduate social work curricula: A study of educators' experience and attitudes. *Journal of Education for Social Work, 18,* 46-54.

Compton, B., & Galaway, B. (1984). *Social work process* (3rd ed.). Homewood, IL: Dorsey.

Constable, R.T. (1984). Social work education: Current issues and future promise. *Social Work, 29,* 366-376.

Council on Social Work Education. (1982). *Curriculum Policy for the Master's Degree and Baccalaureate Degree Programs in Social Work Education,* document No 82-310-0GR. New York: Council on Social Work Education.

Egan, G. (1975). *The skilled helper: A model for systematic helping and interpersonal relating.* Monterey, CA: Brooks-Cole.

Garvin, C.D., & Seabury, B.A. (1984). *Interpersonal practice in social work: Process and procedures.* Englewood Cliffs, NJ: Prentice-Hall.

Germain, C., & Gitterman, A. (1980). *The life model of social work practice.* New York: Columbia University Press.

Green, J. (1982). *Cultural awareness in the human services.* Englewood Cliffs, NJ: Prentice-Hall.

Guzzetta, C. (1982). MSW education: The present state. Unpublished paper, Hunter College. Cited in Hokenstad, M.C., Jr. (1984). Curriculum directions for the 1980s: Implications of the new curriculum policy statement. *Journal of Education for Social Work, 20,* 15-22.

Hartman, A. (1983). Concentrations, specializations and curriculum design in MSW and BSW programs. *Journal of Education for Social Work, 19,* 79-85.

Hepworth, D.H., & Larsen, J. (1982). *Direct social work practice: Theory and skills*. Homewood, IL: Dorsey.

Hokenstad, M.C. (1984). Curriculum directions for the 1980s: Implications of the new curriculum policy statement. *Journal of Education for Social Work, 20*, 15-22.

Hollis, F.E., & Woods, M.E. (1981). *Casework: A psychosocial theory* (3rd ed.). New York: Random House.

Lauderdale, M.L., Grinnell, R.M., Jr., & McMurtry, S.L. (1980). Child welfare curricula in schools of social work; A national study, *Child Welfare, 59*, 531-541.

Leighninger, L. (1980). The generalist-specialist debate in social work. *Social Service Review, 54*, 1-12.

Pincus, A., & Minahan, A. (1973). *Social work practice: Model and method*. Itasca, IL: Peacock.

Ruperstein, H., & Block, M.H. (1982). *Things that matter: Influences on helping relationships*. New York: Macmillan.

Shulman, L. (1984). *The skills of helping* (2nd ed.). Itasca, IL: Peacock.

Allan Edward Barsky

S t u d y   F

Neutrality in Child Protection Mediation

THE RAPID GROWTH of mediation in fields as diverse as divorce mediation and commercial dispute resolution has raised the interest of a growing number of child welfare service providers and scholars interested in finding a more constructive process for developing collaborative service plans with families and youth (Mayer, 1987). Several jurisdictions have already introduced mediators at various levels of the child protection system (Barsky, 1995a; Oran, Creamer, & Libow, 1984; Thoennes, 1994; Savoury, Beals, & Parks, 1995).

Mediation is proposed by some advocates as a more effective method of engaging families in treatment (Bernstein, Campbell, & Sookraj, 1993). Others argue that it could provide major time and cost savings by avoiding protracted court hearings (Morden, 1989). Yet others maintain that mediation provides a basis for empowering families and ensuring that child protection services proceed in a manner that is least intrusive to families and children (Regehr, 1994; Wildgoose, 1987).

Most writings to date have focused either on developing a rationale for using mediation in child protection (Eddy, 1992; Palmer, 1989; Wildgoose, 1987) or on evaluation of various programs (Campbell &

Rodenburgh, 1994; Center for Policy Research, 1992; Golten, 1986; Mayer, 1984; Smith, Maresca, Duffy, Banelis, Handelman, & Dale, 1992; Wildgoose & Maresca, 1994). However, there has been insufficient work describing the process of child protection mediation, and analyzing ways in which mediation can be integrated into child protection services.

Accordingly, this study was designed to provide an in-depth understanding of the process of mediation in child protection, and to identify the essential aspects that contribute to developing more effective working relationships with child welfare clients. This paper focuses on neutrality, one of the primary aspects of child protection "CP" mediation identified in the larger study (Barsky, 1995a).

This study is distinct from prior studies because it entails the use of extensive interviews with family members, as well as with professionals involved in mediation and other CP processes. An analysis of their experiences contributes to the child welfare and mediation literature: (1) by beginning to determine the critical experiences of parties involved in the different processes, (2) by developing a framework delineating the essential aspects of the mediation process that are unique to mediation, and (3) by identifying mediative skills and strategies that can be employed in other areas of child protection services.

DESIGN AND METHODS

In order to develop a better understanding of the dynamics of child protection mediation, this study used naturalistic inquiry methods (Denzin & Lincoln, 1994). A series of exploratory "long interviews" (McCracken, 1988) were conducted with 17 adult family members, mediators, and child protection workers ("CPWs") who had been directly involved in five mediation cases. The primary focus of these interviews was to have research participants discuss what they felt were the critical issues in their experiences with mediation. The researcher also conducted six pre-mediation interviews, and six additional interviews with family members and CPWs from three nonmediation comparison cases. The experiences of the research participants in the pre-mediation interviews and in the nonmediation cases provided the contrast points used in identifying the essential aspects of mediation (Spradley, 1979).

Sample

Mediation cases were sampled on the basis of availability and willingness to participate, from a pool of approximately 30 mediation cases seen by the Center for Child and Family Mediation in Metropolitan Toronto. The Center offers mediation to families from Toronto who are involved in the child protection system. Out of this catchment population, all subjects had to meet the following minimum criteria in order to be eligible for mediation:

- The physical safety of the child was assured (i.e., the child was not in any immediate danger).
- The case involved a legitimate child protection concern (suspicions, evidence, or potential for neglect/abuse), and the question of whether a child was in need of protection was not in issue.
- All parties' participation in the process was voluntary.
- All parties to the actual negotiations were competent to negotiate for themselves (i.e., absence of any condition that rendered the party unable to understand the process, to bargain, or to make his/her interests known; the implications for mediation of the existence of an uncontrolled mental illness, significant retardation, language impediment, substance abuse, etc. were assessed on a case-by-case basis).
- There was an absence of any family violence so severe as to render any of the parties incapable of negotiating due to intimidation.
- There were no outstanding criminal charges related to the issues to be mediated.
- There were no ongoing family assessments. (Barsky, 1992)

Although it was not possible (due to client confidentiality) to directly collect data on the nonstudy cases, the study cases had a similar profile to cases described in a prior evaluation of the Center (Wildgoose & Maresca, 1994). The study cases involved a range of child protection issues including neglect, abuse, wardship, access, and supervision. Parties involved in this research study included CPWs, parents, grandparents, extended family members, and foster parents.

The number of mediation sessions in the study sample ranged from three to eight, similar to the average number of sessions used by the Center. The study sample included both cases that settled and cases that did not settle in mediation; however, the levels of conflict in some of the nonstudy cases that did not settle may have been higher than the levels of conflict in the study sample.

None of the cases proceeded to trial following mediation, whereas the Center has had cases that have had to go to trial. Given this limitation, it may be inappropriate to generalize from this study about cases that cannot be resolved in mediation and need to be tried in court. Although the nature and size of the sample do mean that any generalization of the results of this study must be made with caution, the main purposes of this study—to explore the experiences of parties involved in child protection mediation and to explore whether they are unique to this process—were not compromised by the nature of the sample that was actually drawn.

In terms of demographics of research participants, most families involved in both the mediation and nonmediation cases were headed by a single mother who was either on social assistance or earning less than $30,000 per annum. All but one family had either one or two children. These demographics are consistent with the general population of families involved in child protection mediation in Toronto.

The sample of nonmediated cases was drawn purposively on a case-by-case basis by having CPWs from the mediation sample identify matching cases from their own caseloads. Selection was done to ensure that the comparison cases matched the mediation cases in terms of demographic profiles, type and severity of maltreatment, placement status, and level of involvement by participants in the case-planning process. In terms of ethnicity, families in the mediation sample included people from European, African, and mixed Euro-African families. All of the families in the nonmediation sample came from Euro-Canadian backgrounds.

Matching for ethnicity was not prioritized, because both mediators and child protection workers suggested that the most important factor to consider was the type of intervention used in the nonmediation cases. Some types of interventions in the child protection process engender philosophies related to those which underpin mediation: e.g., solution-focused therapy, case conferencing, and plan of care meetings (Tjaden, 1994; Bernstein, Campbell & Sookraj, 1993). Accordingly, in order to explore whether mediation is qualitatively different from other child protection processes, the investigator tried to select comparison cases in which mediation-like interventions were employed.

Data Collection

Semi-structured interviews were conducted with family members, CPWs, and mediators one interviewee at a time (except in one family, where the parents asked to be interviewed together so that they would be more at ease). Each interview was 50 to 90 minutes in duration and was conducted at a location of convenience to the interviewee. Question guides were used to ensure that all relevant questions and topics were raised. Interviews were conducted flexibly in order to focus the study on the participants' perspectives on mediation and the child protection process, rather than limit the study's preconceived problem areas. Questions for the interview guide were developed from:

- Research studies on CP mediation from the Denver/Boulder project (Mayer, 1987; Pearson, Thoennes, Mayer, & Golten, 1986).
- Pilot research studies on CP mediation completed in Toronto (Morden, 1989; Smith et al., 1992).
- Research studies on child protection cases without mediation (Shulman, 1991).

Additional data were obtained from mediation case files and data being collected for evaluative research on the Center (Morden, 1989). These data helped to supplement and check data gathered in the qualitative interviews.

Ethical Issues

Because this research study dealt with human research participants, the proposal underwent the ethics review procedure required by the University of Toronto School of Graduate Studies. The following ethical guidelines were established and followed:

- Participation in both the mediation and the research study components was strictly voluntary. Participants were permitted to withdraw from the research study, without obligation to provide justification (in one situation where there was initial consent to participate, consent was later withdrawn and information from that case was excluded from the research study).

- No one was denied mediation on the basis that he or she refused to participate in the research study component.
- The researcher did not have access to confidential information concerning any child protection cases, unless and until consents had been received from all of the relevant parties (especially, the parents and the child protection agency).
- The researcher took all reasonable measures to limit access to the data, even in coded form, on a need-to-know basis. Transcription of tapes was done by the primary researcher and one typist. Names and other identifying information in the tapes were altered in the written transcripts to protect the identities of the participants. The researcher stored all of the data in his private office.
- Participants were given notice that anonymity could not be absolutely guaranteed, because research records do not have privileged status under the law and, while it was unlikely, could be subpoenaed for a court trial. As a precondition of participation in the research study, participants were asked to sign an agreement not to call the researcher or any of his documentation for use in any further child protection proceedings.
- Identifying information was separated from the research data, and no identifying information was included in any published material resulting from this study.
- Once the final thesis and oral review were successfully completed, all tapes were erased.

Data Analysis

The interviews were audiotaped and transcribed. In a situation where a parent asked not to be taped, written notes were used to develop a transcript. Each interview was read, reread, and analyzed as it was completed, rather than waiting to analyze all of the interviews together. Key themes and patterns from the interviewees' perspectives were identified from the transcripts (Lincoln & Guba, 1985; Taylor & Bogden, 1984). The interview guides were altered for subsequent interviews in order to further explore important topics and perspectives raised by interviewees that were not originally identified by the researcher. McCracken's five-stage model for data analysis was employed (McCracken, 1988). The transcribed texts were processed for analysis with the *Ethnograph* computer software package (Seidel & Clark, 1984).

Four different types of comparisons were made between interviews:

- First, each interview was compared to an interview of another party from the same child protection case (e.g., a parent's interview could be compared to interviews of the mediator and the CPW on the case, etc.). Different participants in the same mediation or child protection process provided different perspectives and experiences.
- Second, interviews from one case were compared to interviews from other cases, but from the same group of cases (i.e., another mediation case or another nonmediation case).
- Third, interviews from pre-mediation were compared to interviews from post-mediation.
- Finally, interviews from one group of cases were compared to interviews from the other group of cases (e.g., mediation cases compared to nonmediation cases).

Coincidences and contrasts in the data were noted in memoranda that were generated at each stage of the analysis.

Lincoln & Guba's (1985) method for establishing trustworthiness was used throughout the study. "Credibility," "transferability," "dependability," and "confirmability" (the qualitative research equivalents of internal validity, external validity, reliability, and objectivity) were each considered.

The researcher operationalized credibility through the use of the following techniques:

- **Triangulation of data**: Cross-checking data and interpretations through the use of multiple data sources, methods, investigators, or theories. The primary sources used for this purpose included data collected from different participants (mediators, CPWs, parents, etc.), through qualitative interviews, evaluative instruments, and case progress notes. In addition, one mediation case was audiotaped in its entirety, allowing for triangulation in this case. Multiple researchers could have been used for the purposes of triangulation, but they are not necessary if there are other sources. Since the researcher's dissertation was intended to be an independent piece of research, multiple researchers were not used. The following analysis, however, does triangulate data in terms of checking whether facts collected are consistent with theory and findings in the literature.

- **Member checking**: Correcting, verifying, and challenging the soundness of the researcher's findings, constructions, and interpretations with the persons who participated in the original interviews.

- **Peer debriefing**: An external check employed by systematically talking through research experiences, findings, and decisions (for the purposes of catharsis, challenge, design of next steps, and legitimization) with noninvolved professional peers. Consultation with mediators from the Center and with the thesis committee were used on an ongoing basis, as they were most familiar with the topics under study. The researcher has also presented this research study at a number of professional conferences, and has solicited feedback from peers in other jurisdictions across North America and Australia.

- **Negative case analysis:** A process of refining working hypotheses (to try to account for all known cases, without exception or with only a reasonable level of exceptions) as more and more data become available.

- **Referential adequacy:** Checking preliminary findings and interpretations against the transcripts and other raw data.

- **Reflexive journals:** The use of reflexive journals that display the researcher's mind processes, philosophical position, and bases of decision about the inquiry. (Lincoln & Guba, 1985)

Two other methods for ensuring credibility—prolonged engagement and persistent observation—were not used, due to pragmatic considerations. Given the level of personal, emotional, and legal concerns in CP cases, prolonged engagement and persistent observation would be too intrusive and too disruptive of the child protection process to warrant their use. Some difficulties with trust and openness were identified in some of the research interviews, which may have been alleviated if the researcher had had a longer period engagement.

In particular, some of the professionals were hesitant to say anything that could be interpreted as shedding a negative light on any of their colleagues (e.g., questioning competence or clinical orientation). Some parents and workers also tended to cast themselves in a positive light (e.g., in terms of responsibility for the conflict between the family and the child protection system).

Each of these tendencies was understandable from the participants' perspectives. Other researchers have decided not to interview family members, because of the "reluctance of many to be candid or critical... concerned about being cooperative" (Center for Policy Research, 1992, pp. 13-14). Since the purpose of the present research study was to gain an understanding of mediation from the participants' perspectives, interviewing family members was essential. In order to take these concerns into account, the following guidelines were followed in interviewing and analyzing the data:

- The researcher reassured the participants that their anonymity would be maintained. One concession that this required was that the researcher could not provide fully detailed descriptions of each case in writing up this analysis. Data had to be separated from each individual case, so that people from within the child protection system could not identify who said what.
- Questions implying judgment—such as whether mediation or another intervention is "good" or "bad"—were avoided.
- In analyzing the data, an evaluation of the effectiveness of mediation or other interventions was not inferred.

In terms of *transferability*, a "thick description" is required in order to enable someone interested in this research study to make an informed judgment about the transferability of the knowledge (Lincoln & Guba, 1985). The depth of description in the findings section is intended to fulfill this requirement. The description of the research sample above can also be used in order to assess the transferability of conclusions from this research study. Finally, the reader may be referred to other CP mediation research that has been written up by the Center (Morden, 1989; Wildgoose & Maresca, 1994), or to literature that describes similar models (e.g., Campbell & Rodenburgh, 1994; Hogan, 1993). The Project Report by Wildgoose and Maresca (1994) provides a detailed description of the program and also provides 23 individual case summaries.

Throughout the process of inquiry, the researcher maintained thorough files stored on computer and on paper. This audit trail included the following:

- Proposal, ethics review, and comprehensive paper (identifying literature, the researcher's understanding of the literature, the initial course of action, methods, questions and consent forms).
- Audiotapes of the interviews (erased upon completion of the author's dissertation).
- Transcriptions of the audiotapes, with identifying information removed.

- Memoranda and notes on cases, interviews, and dissertation committee meetings (including successive stages of coding and development of themes, reflective memoranda, tentative hypotheses, and notes of how decisions were made concerning data collection).
- Coded interviews using the *Ethnograph*.
- Searches of specific themes.
- Successive drafts of the analysis and findings.

Mediator files that have been reviewed for the purposes of triangulation would not be available to the auditor since this includes identifying information for which the parties have not given consent to be viewed by an external auditor.

Retention of this audit trail allows for *dependability* to be checked through the use of an "auditor" to examine whether the process of inquiry was carried out in a way that is consistent with good professional practice. The audit trail also enabled a check for *confirmability* by examining whether the products (the findings, interpretations, and recommendations) were internally consistent and supported by the raw data (the taped and transcribed interviews). The transparency of method and systematic record keeping used in this study allow for the analysis to be followed and replicated (Denzin & Lincoln, 1994; Lincoln & Guba, 1985).

Data collected from the eight cases comprised 26 interviews (not including member checks). At an average of 22 pages of transcript per interview, the 26 interviews produced approximately 550 pages of transcript. During the initial stage of analysis, the researcher attempted to hit as many themes as the participants' data indicated. This resulted in a broad base of 92 themes. Many of these themes overlapped, and some of them did not prove to be significant in later analysis. However, since the purpose of the study was to look at mediation from the participants' perspectives, it was beneficial to start with a broad identification of themes. While the number of initial themes was difficult to manage, as soon as the process of distilling themes begins, there is greater chance of misconstruing the meanings of the primary data and losing some of the distinctions. Reduction was necessary in order to allow for meaningful discussion and conceptualization of the participants' experiences.

The initial themes were loosely categorized into nine pools: (1) Intentions and Concerns of the Parties, (2) Mediation Interventions, (3) Dynamics between the Parties, (4) Appropriateness for Mediation, (5)

Comparisons Made by the Parties, (6) Roles of the Parties, (7) Factors Affecting Decisions, (8) Outcomes, and (9) Impact of the Research Study. These pools provided a framework for the full write-up of this study (Barsky, 1995a).

The next stage of analysis led to the identification of the so-called "essential aspects" of the mediation process. These themes were derived in part from the aspects of mediation that mediation participants identified as being most important. There were also certain recurring themes that the parties did not specifically state were the most important, but which emerged implicitly as defining features of their experiences in the mediation process. One of the difficulties in this process was to try to separate out themes that the interviewer may have suggested through the use of leading questions. Thus, it was useful to look at the early portions of the interview where the interviewer asked more general questions.

Eventually, ten distinct essential elements were discerned: alliance, bringing parties together, facilitating communication, keeping peace, developing options, enhancing understanding, focusing the parties, contracting, neutrality, and fairness. These themes do not encompass all of the original themes, but do cover a broad spectrum. In order for the analysis to be manageable, similar themes were regrouped into more general themes. For example, a number of narrower themes from the Mediation Interventions grouping (e.g., clarify, share information) were placed into a broader theme, facilitating communication. The written analysis of facilitating communication reflects its components, as identified in the initial labeling process. The analysis continued by drawing contrasts and comparisons among the original data, the development of themes and information from the literature.

FINDINGS

As noted above, ten essential aspects of mediation were identified in the original research study (Barsky, 1995a). For the purposes of illustration, the following discussion focuses on just one of these aspects—neutrality. For ease of reference, the first initial of each participant's pseudonym corresponds with the first initial of the participant's role: P = Parent, C = Child, W = Worker, M = Mediator, and G = Grandparent.

Mediators, family members, and CPWs each described the mediator as a "neutral" or "impartial" third party. All three groups tended to rate mediator neutrality as a very important element of the mediation process. Upon exploring further what these parties meant by "neutrality," four themes emerged: not siding; absence of preexisting bias; absence of decision-making authority; and no stake in a specific type of outcome.

One of the most consistent themes across cases and parties was the understanding that a mediator could be neutral by *not siding with one party more than any other*. Family members provided the following three examples of how the mediator would treat everybody equally, giving everyone the same opportunity to speak and listening to all sides:

> [The mediator] never sided with us, or not really sided with us and not sided with Children's Aid workers. She always tried to keep it into a medium... At the beginning of every meeting she would say, "Okay, well, I am not here to take your side or your side. I will sit and listen to both sides..."

> Melanie would go talk to the [foster] family, come talk to us, but she was really on nobody's side, so it was just a matter of listening...

> [Mediators need to be] nonbiased and represent both sides equally...

These types of sentiments were mirrored by CPWs, who spoke of the mediator's asking all parties for their points of view and giving everyone's input the same treatment.

> Martha had the ability to treat everybody as equal around the table, to give no one person's ideas or voice more than the others. So it becomes presented more on an equal footing. And everybody got their fair air time. Everyone's opinion got heard...

> A neutral person, someone that sort of will work for both parties, doesn't work for one side or the other.

> Mindy's neutrality was... appearing to give everyone equal footing and to consider everybody in the decisions, asking everybody's opinions about a decision. [Mindy was] moving us along, but not appearing to come down on one side or the other.

The mediators were also conscious of how aligning or even appearing to align with one side would compromise their neutrality. If they met individually with one party, then they would be sure to meet individually with all of the parties. The mediators generally held the mediation sessions at their own offices, rather than at the CPW's office or at the family's home, so as to avoid the appearance of siding with one party. They also tried to ensure that everybody's voice was heard within the mediation sessions.

Absence of a preexisting bias was a second concept identified by some of the family members, CPWs, and mediators as one of the components of neutrality. One uncle suggested that the mediator was able to treat the parties as equals because of the fact that the mediator had no prior history with the family:

> We went to somebody who knew nothing about the case, because she met with people and heard their perceptions, and then came to the table to talk to us as equal partners.

Neutrality in this sense meant that the parties did not see the mediators as being partial to a certain type of outcome.

Since most of the cases dealt with by the Center were already in court, the CPWs were generally parties to the court action. In contrast, the mediators had no standing in the court proceedings. One mediator suggested that not being a party to the action was critical to her neutrality.

CPWs in particular believed that one of the reasons that a mediator may be perceived as more neutral (as compared to a CPW) was the fact that the mediator had no prior history with the family. Although CPWs attempted to be open-minded and unbiased about how to resolve conflicts with the family, some CPWs acknowledged that they sometimes became entrenched in a particular position.

Some of the mediators also agreed that CPWs may become locked into a position, making it difficult for them to negotiate a new arrangement with the family. In two mediation cases, certain family members perceived that the CPW had aligned with other family members. Therefore, even though the primary conflict was between various family members, the CPWs were not seen by the family as neutral mediators. A similar situation occurred in a nonmediation case where the CPW attempted to mediate between a mother and two sets of grandparents. One of the grandmothers felt that the CPW was biased against her, making it difficult for her to accept the CPW in a mediator's role.

In some cases, CPWs and parents had asked the mediators specifically about their affiliations. Family members and their lawyers were particularly interested in whether the mediator was employed by the child protection agency, the court, or other government sources. Some family members were satisfied with mediator neutrality if the mediator were not employed by the protection agency; others believed that all government agencies were the same and questioned whether the mediator was really any different from someone from the protection agency:

> I think [my mother, Genny] does believe mediation is the same process as Children's Aid... She has nothing against Melanie, but it's the same process, dealing with the same people, the same government people you're dealing with. It's just that somebody else is there as a mediator.

The concerns that family members had about the affiliations of their mediator were similar to concerns that they had about judges. In one case, the worker noted that the mother questioned the judge's neutrality: "Patricia doesn't fully trust a judge, and to this day thinks that a judge works for the Children's Aid." Over the course of mediation, Patricia developed an understanding about the mediator's independence from the protection agency. However, she continued to doubt the judge's neutrality.

In four mediation cases, family members believed that the protection agency had betrayed them in the past. Regardless of the worker's attempts to show the family good faith, the family members could not see the CPW as neutral. To the extent that a mediator could demonstrate that she was not part of the agency, the family believed that the mediator would not be biased in the agency's favor.

Accordingly, there was a sense among family members that if the mediator were not directly connected with the agency, then the mediator could be accepted as more neutral. Family members who understood that the mediator was not bound by the same regulations as the protection agency also seemed to have more faith in the neutrality of the mediator:

> Wendy... has her regulations and guidelines that she has to follow. By her explaining anything to me, I would have a little bit of doubt as to the sincerity of it because of her regulations, whereas Melanie has no involvement. So whatever she's going to do is going to be better for everybody involved. So, I would tend to not question as much what she says...

Some CPWs knew the mediators from prior cases where the mediators had acted as lawyers for one of the parties. As long as the mediator had not acted in the same case, this did not tend to cause grave concerns about the mediator's neutrality from the family's perspective. In one case where the CPW knew the mediator from when she worked as a lawyer for the agency, the CPW initially found it hard to see the mediator as neutral. The CPW expected that the mediator would tend to side with her. However, when the mediator really treated the family in a neutral manner, this invoked strong feelings for the CPW. The CPW believed the father was a pedophile. When the mediator treated him with respect and without judgment, the CPW found this hard to accept. The CPW thought, "Oh my God. How can she believe him." The mediator was attempting to demonstrate that she was hearing what the father said. When the mediator did not challenge his statements, the CPW felt this indicated that she was believing what he was saying. The CPW eventually understood that the mediator needed to respond this way in order to maintain neutrality.

Both CPWs and mediators suggested that critical to mediator neutrality was the fact that mediators *did not have any decision-making authority:*

> CPW: Maureen was not there making the decision… And that's where my role is different, because I have to make a decision and she doesn't.

Whereas CPWs have the mandate and power to remove children from their homes, initiate a child protection hearing, and make recommendations to the court, mediators have no legitimate power to impose decisions on the parties and have no direct reporting obligations to the court. This concern was not as apparent from the responses of family members. The concern, however, was implicit in their references to wanting someone who was not biased and did not take sides. For family members, their explicit concern was not so much about a person having decision-making power, but whether the person with power was biased or sided against them.

According to one mediator, family members entering the mediation process often "don't know the mediator from Adam." Most of them are unfamiliar with the mediation profession, as well as with the mediator personally. As a matter of practice, the mediators explained to all of the parties that they did not have the power to impose decisions upon them:

> One of the things that I do is I tell them that I'm not an employee of the Children's Aid Society, so that I'm not connected with that organization. And then I tell them that I don't make any decisions. You know, that I'm not going to do a report. I'm not going to talk to anybody else, you know, outside of research, about the case. I don't get to make any decisions. And if they, at any point, think that it's not working, they can walk without consequence. I'm not the one that they should be convincing.

The CPW in a nonmediation case confirmed that one of the characteristics that makes a mediator neutral is that mediators do not have the mandate or power to advance a particular outcome:

> Well, I had the authority that I could, you know, I mean the court makes the final decision, but I think we really make the final decision as to whether or not the kids go home. In terms of assessment, we advise the court. So Paul knew I had the authority. So I think that's the major difference. You know, mediators are neutral. We're not neutral. We're certainly fighting for those kids, to get the best that they can in terms of planning and care... [Paul] sees me as having power and authority, definitely.

In one case, Wilma noted that while her supportive role was amenable to neutrality, she also had an authoritative role that ran counter to neutrality. In that role, she was required to make decisions that would have an impact on the family:

> Through Patricia's eyes, the mediator is someone who's separate, not part of the agency. You know, and through her eyes the agency is supposed to be biased against her... Although we try to wear two hats, I mean I try to be the supportive worker, but I also have to be the protection worker, and that's the double hats, the authoritarian figure and the supportive one, right? When the authoritarian figure comes out, which usually happens when you go to court, the client can't see you as supportive, and really you're not supportive to what they want, so that's where the mediator comes in. Because they can be in the middle... And that's where my role is different. Because I have to make a decision, and she doesn't. I could be wrong. You know, that's where my lack of experience with mediation comes in.

The final keystone of neutrality was whether the mediator had a *stake in a specific outcome*. This concern was also identified most specifically by mediators and CPWs. One CPW referred to the fact that a mediator has nothing to win or lose in the situation. Similarly, the mediators tended to agree that a mediator had no stake in the outcome of the mediation other than trying to ensure that no one thinks (at the end of the process) that the mediator took sides. The mediators were concerned about the process being fair, but had no vested interest.

One CPW suggested that once CPWs adopt a certain position, maintaining that position may become a vested interest. She suggested that mediators were neutral because they never had to decide whose position was more credible or better for the child:

> I think sometimes we get entrenched in our positions and have a hard time thinking that something could be different. Sometimes we get what feels like very

far along in the court process, and we become entrenched. And whether that be the Official Guardian or the Children's Aid, I think it makes it hard for that person to act as the mediator... I think sometimes while we do an awful lot of mediation, knowing or not knowing that it's in court, and also that there are other resources and all sorts of things. I think when it gets into where people are really entrenched in positions, then I think we, whether it's clients or lawyers, people don't see us as being able to be the mediator, because we have a very vested interest. And here comes somebody who has no vested interest. Maybe that's what I was trying to get at when I was talking about the neutrality. *Mindy had no vested interest, except wanting to try to help us work this out. But she had no vested interest in one opinion being better than the other, or more credible or better for the child.* And so I think that's what makes the difference. (emphasis added)

Wanda said she expected a mediator to be an "objective person" to help them work through their dispute. She defined "objective" as follows:

Somebody who's listening to both sides and, and has nothing to win or lose in the whole situation. They can just reflect on what is being said. And, and point out different areas that maybe neither [side has seen before], 'cause I'm involved and maybe Patricia's involved...

In Case 6, the parties specifically wanted a mediator to meet with the child, Charles, "as a neutral person, not as someone with a vested interest." Previously, the family had heard different messages from the foster parents and various workers about what Charles wanted. The family did not trust what they were saying. The family believed that when the foster mother asked Charles whether he wanted to spend time with his uncles, she may have influenced what Charles said because she did not want Charles to spend time with them. The family also believed that the CPW wanted to keep the foster mother happy. The family had more faith in having the mediator convey Charles' wishes, because the mediator did not have a stake in a particular outcome:

In this case, one of my specific roles was going to be to meet with Charles as a neutral person, not as someone with a vested interest or any interest really in what he had to say. Up until this point they were hearing things from the worker, Wendy, and from the foster mother, Barb, and they weren't hearing things, and which wasn't necessarily consistent with what they were, had been hearing in the past from Charles directly. And so I think, yes, in this case, it was a little bit more important than even the other cases to establish, reinforce my position of neutrality.

Melanie suggested that the only stake that she had as a mediator was to try to ensure that the parties felt that the process was fair to each of them:

> I have a stake as the mediator in ensuring that nobody thinks that I'm taking sides. That's my biggest stake... You want to be able to put out options for people, so that they know what's possible and even to stimulate brainstorming. You know, I'll throw out three, you throw out three, you throw out three sort of thing. So that's the stake that I have — not alienating anybody, and making sure that everybody feels that it's fair. You know, if somebody walks out feeling that it was unfair or that they were coerced, then to me, I have failed. They can walk out without an agreement; that happens all the time. There's nothing that says it always has to work. Maybe it's better that they don't walk out with an agreement, but if anybody walks out feeling that it was unfair, that's when I think I've failed as a mediator.

The definitions of neutrality provided by the parties are generally consistent with definitions in the literature. A proposed set of national standards for court-connected mediation programs in the United States, for instance, defined impartiality as freedom from favoritism or bias either by appearance, word or by action, and a commitment to serve all of the parties as opposed to a single party. This definition covers three of the four categories of neutrality identified in the current research study: absence of preexisting bias, having no stake in the outcome, and not siding with one party.

The fourth category of neutrality, the absence of decision-making authority, is not generally included in definitions of neutrality. Mediators are generally assumed not to have decision-making authority, aside from the issue of neutrality. In the context of CP cases, the issue of decision-making authority has different connotations than in other fields of mediation. Professionals mandated under the child protection system are generally charged with the responsibility for assessing risks to children and taking appropriate measures to redress them. Child protection mediators are an exception. They are not mandated to make decisions regarding protection concerns. The parties involved in this study viewed this absence of decision-making responsibility as contributing to the neutrality of the mediator.

By refraining from expressing opinions and from making decisions, the mediators avoided any sort of alignment with the position of one party or the other. Further, this helped to ensure that the parties saw the role of a mediator as different from that of the CPW. This also differentiated them from the role of a judge. Although judges may be neutral in term of having no preexisting bias, they do have decision-making authority and they are bound by legal principles.

Two other aspects of neutrality were identified that did not fit into the four categories. One CPW said that neutrality required that the mediator establish ground rules and follow through on them. Another CPW said the neutrality required that the mediator be up front about the issues that needed to be dealt with. Although these are not generally ideas associated with the concept of neutrality, they are dynamics that help parties to gain and maintain trust with the mediator.

LIMITATIONS

While this in-depth qualitative study produced an unexpected wealth of material on the processes of mediation in child welfare settings, several limitations in the design of the study must be carefully considered before drawing conclusions from the findings. As with many small sample naturalistic studies, caution should be used in generalizing the findings beyond the study sample. The study was carried out in only one agency using a specific pilot mediation model. In addition the sample was not systematically drawn and did not appear to include some of the higher conflict cases seen in the program.

A second important limitation with the study is the small number of pre-mediation interviews. Although pre-mediation interviews run the risk of influencing the process itself, they provided an interesting contrast point for the analysis.

Finally, identification of a matched comparison group proved to be more difficult than anticipated. The investigators and participants had difficulty coming to agreement about what would constitute an equivalent nonmediated process, and at what point in the process should the interviews take place. Finding an equivalent group was particularly difficult given that the mediation program was a pilot program benefiting from the effects of a novel, voluntary, and well-staffed demonstration program.

CONCLUSIONS

Child protection mediation is a peculiar use of mediation, given that one of the clients is a professional who traditionally assumes a mediation role in her own work. When suspicions of child abuse or neglect are brought to the attention of a child protection agency, the assigned worker is mandated to investigate and intervene in order to ensure that the child is not at risk. In order to achieve these ends, the worker can draw on a range of generalist social work roles: enabler, broker, advocate, activist, mediator, negotiator, educator, initiator, coordinator and group facilitator (Zastrow, 1995). According to Zastrow (1995):

> The mediator role involves intervention in disputes between parties to help them find compromises, reconcile differences, or reach mutually satisfactory agreements... A mediator remains neutral, not siding with either party in the dispute. Mediators make sure they understand the positions of the parties. They help clarify positions, recognize miscommunication, and help the parties present their cases clearly. (p. 19)

In the context of child protection, a worker could mediate between disputing family members about how they will share responsibility for a child's needs. Similarly, a worker could mediate between parents and foster parents about how and when the parents will spend time with the child. But is a child protection worker truly able to function as a neutral third party? For CP mediation to have value as a distinct intervention, it needs to be defined in a way that is different from just "good clinical practice" by CPWs. Otherwise, a CPW could fulfill the role, making the use of an independent mediator redundant (Barsky, 1995b). One of the major findings from the present research study was that neutrality does differentiate the role of a mediator from the role of a CPW.

If neutrality means having someone who listens to all sides and who can view a situation with an open mind, then the question arises about whether a CPW could be neutral in these respects. CPWs who have received sufficient training ought to be able to listen to all sides and treat everyone's views with equal respect. In fact, these are generally accepted standards for professional social workers. CPWs may become locked in a certain position or may become overidentified with one client to the exclusion of others. However, if a CPW does lose this sense of neutrality, the agency can assign a new (more neutral) worker to try to work things out. The worker does not necessarily have to be from outside of the agency. In fact, changing workers for this purpose was used in at least two of the research cases.

Of the four themes that comprise neutrality, the two that separate mediators from CPWs are the concepts of "absence of authority" and "having no stake in a particular outcome." The role of a mediator can be distinguished from that of a CPW by virtue of the fact that the mediator has responsibility for establishing a collaborative problem-solving process, without incurring the task of determining the best substantive outcome (Mayer, 1989). The mediator helps the parties develop their own mutual understanding about what needs to be done for the safety and welfare of the children.

In contrast, CPWs are mandated to carry out the provisions of the child protection legislation. While they must first try to resolve protection issues on a consensual basis, they are vested with the authority and power to secure the protection of children on a nonvoluntary basis. They also have the authority to make recommendations to the court with regard to ongoing intervention on a nonvoluntary basis. This creates a tendency for workers and clients to act as partisans in negotiating with one another:

> Each has a different definition of the problem and different loyalties, commitments and investments in outcome. (Murdach, 1980, p. 458)

Neutrality is bound by perception. Many people have preconceived ideas about CPWs. Even if CPWs strive to be open minded, flexible and nonjudgmental, they have great difficulty overcoming preconceptions of family members that contradict these efforts. Although some family members who participated in the research study originally viewed mediators with suspicion, family members tended to trust mediators as neutral parties within the first or second session. Because mediators were able to secure the trust of parties in ways unavailable to CPWs, mediators were able to move the parties to consensus in situations where collaboration and agreement had previously eluded the parties.

The differences between mediation and other child protection processes do not suggest that mediation is an inherently better process in all situations. For instance, mediators were able to build trust in some cases because family members saw them as independent of the child protection system. However, in some of the nonmediation cases, family members did not necessarily want to work with an independent professional. The CPW may have built up a positive working relationship through strategies unavailable to mediators (e.g., advocacy for the family with other systems; familiarity through intensive work over a longer period of time; provision of concrete services; and building trust by following through on successive agreements).

Further, some family members wanted an intervenor who would make decisions. They wanted clear-cut solutions more than participation in the decision-making process. In some cases that had gone to court over an extended period, family members were frustrated by the lack of finality. Mediation does not necessarily conclude with an agreement. If the parties do not want agreement or if agreement is not possible, then mediation is not their optimal choice.

The fact that neutrality is an essential aspect of CP mediation has significant implications for research and practice. Further study is needed to identify the limits of neutrality:

- What are the mediator's obligations in a situation where treating both parties equally would allow the more powerful party (usually the CPW) take unfair advantage of the other party?
- What are the mediator's obligations in a situation where the mediator believes that the parties are coming to an agreement that will put a child at undue risk of abuse or neglect?

For CP mediators, this research study identifies four components of neutrality to take into account: not siding; absence of preexisting bias; absence of decision-making authority; and no stake in a specific type of outcome. Each of these elements contributes to the mediator's ability to establish trust with the parties, which subsequently helps them work toward a consensual resolution of their conflict.

Although the present research study was not intended to evaluate the effectiveness of CP mediation, research participants tended to volunteer positive feedback on their experiences in mediation. In particular, mediation helped them resolve issues without going to court, helped build a more positive relationship between family members and the agency, and gave all parties a sense of being heard and treated fairly. CP mediation is not a panacea, as noted by the frustration of some parties in cases that did not settle. However, given the efficacy of mediation in this small sample of cases, further study is warranted.

REFERENCES

Barsky, A.E. (1992). Mediation in child protection cases: Managing mandate, authority and power, with self-determination, choice and autonomy. Comprehensive doctoral paper. University of Toronto, Faculty of Social Work.

Barsky, A.E. (1995a). Essential aspects of mediation in child protection cases. Doctoral dissertation, University of Toronto Faculty of Social Work, Toronto.

Barsky, A.E. (1995b). Mediation in child protection cases. In H.H. Irving & M. Benjamin (Eds.), *Family mediation: Contemporary issues* (pp. 377-406). Newbury Park, CA: Sage.

Bernstein, M., Campbell, J., & Sookraj, N. (1993). *Transforming child welfare services in the 90's.* Unpublished paper, Catholic Children's Aid Society of Metropolitan Toronto.

Campbell, J., & Rodenburgh, M. (1994). *Mediation pilot project evaluation.* Unpublished program evaluation, Ministry of Social Services, Victoria, BC.

Center for Policy Research, Denver. (1992). *Alternatives to adjudication in child abuse and neglect cases.* Alexandria, VA: State Justice Institute.

Denzin, N.K., & Lincoln, Y.S. (Eds.). (1994). *Handbook of qualitative research.* Newbury Park, CA: Sage.

Eddy, W.A. (1992). *Mediation in San Diego's Dependency Court: A balancing solution for a system under fire?* Unpublished paper, University of San Diego School of Law.

Golten, M.M. (1986). *Child Protection Mediation Project.* Final report. Denver: CDR Associates.

Hogan, J. (1993, July). Mediating child welfare cases. Paper presented at the Academy of Family Mediators Conference, Washington, DC.

Lincoln, Y.S., & Guba, E.G. (1985). *Naturalistic inquiry.* Newbury Park, CA: Sage.

Mayer, B. (Ed.). (1984). *Child Protection Project Manual.* Denver: CDR Associates.

Mayer, B. (1987). *Mediation and compliance in child protection.* Unpublished doctoral dissertation, University of Denver.

Mayer, B. (1989). Mediation in child protection cases: The impact of third party intervention on compliance attitudes. *Mediation Quarterly, 24,* 89-106.

McCracken, G. (1988). *The long interview.* Newbury Park, CA: Sage.

Morden, P. (1989). *Child Protection Mediation Demonstration Project.* Research proposal, Children's Aid Society Foundation of Metropolitan Toronto.

Murdach, A.D. (1980, November). Bargaining and persuasion with nonvoluntary clients. *Social Work,* 458-461.

Oran, H., Creamer, J., & Libow, J. (1984). *Dependence Mediation Court Project: The first seven months* (Evaluation Report). Los Angeles: Supreme Court.

Palmer, S.E. (1989). Mediation in child protection cases: An alternative to the adversarial system. *Child Welfare, 68,* 21-31.

Pearson, J., Thoennes, N., Mayer, B., & Golten, M.M. (1986). Mediation of child welfare cases. *Family Law Quarterly, 20,* 303-320.

Regehr, C. (1994). The use of empowerment in child custody mediation. *Family Mediation Quarterly, 11,* 361-372.

Savoury, G.R., Beals, H.L., & Parks, J.M. (1995). Mediation in child protection: Facilitating the resolution of disputes. *Child Welfare, 74,* 743-762.

Seidel, J.V., & Clark, J.A. (1984). *The Ethnograph:* A computer program for the analysis of qualitative data. *Qualitative Sociology, 7,* 110-125.

Shulman, L. (1991). *Interactional social work practice: Toward an empirical theory.* Itasca, IL: Peacock.

Smith, R., Maresca, J., Duffy, M., Banelis, N., Handelman, C., & Dale, N. (1992). *Mediation in child protection: Limited or limitless possibilities.* Unpublished report, Demonstration Project of the Children's Aid Society of Metropolitan Toronto.

Spradley, J.P. (1979). *The ethnographic interview.* New York: Holt, Rinehart & Winston.

Taylor, S.J., & Bogdan, R. (1984). *Introduction to qualitative research methods* (2nd ed.). New York: John Wiley.

Thoennes, N. (1994). Child protection mediation in the juvenile court. *The Judge's Journal, 33,* 14-19, 40-43.

Tjaden, P.G. (1994). Dispute resolution in child protection cases. *Negotiation Journal, 10,* 373-390.

Wildgoose, J. (1987). Alternative dispute resolution of child protection cases. *Canadian Journal of Family Law, 6,* 61-84.

Wildgoose, J., & Maresca, J. (1994). *Report on the Centre for Child and Family Mediation, Toronto.* Kitchener, ON: Network-Interaction for Conflict Resolution.

Zastrow, C. (1995). *The practice of social work* (5th ed.). Belmont, CA: Wadsworth.

Yvonne A. Unrau
Kathryn Conley Wehrmann

Study G

Evaluation of a Home-Based Rural Literacy Program[1]

Evidence about the effectiveness of family literacy programs is sparse in comparison to the large number of programs in operation. Canada and the United States have comparable distribution patterns for literacy levels (OECD & Statistics Canada, 1995). With respect to prose literacy, which requires readers to understand and use information from text such as editorials, stories, poems, and fiction, 42.2 percent of Canada's population and 46.6 percent of the US population fall below the minimum desirable level of literacy (OECD & Statistics Canada, 1995).

Poor literacy skills have somber consequences for individuals and society alike; particularly since literacy has an integral role with most daily activities. Reading road signs, writing notes, reading food and drug labels, and reading instructions are just a few literacy activities that most citizens encounter daily. While it is possible for people with poor literacy skills to successfully maneuver through a literate world (Bishop,

[1] This research study was funded by the National Literacy Secretariat, Canada

1991), it is more likely that they will experience unemployment and poverty (OECD & Statistics Canada, 1995).

Parenting behavior, parent-child interactions, inter-generational attitudes toward literacy, and parent attitudes toward education all have positive relationships with literacy skills (Cronan, Cruz, & Arriaga, 1996). In other words, families characterized by "high scores" in each of these four areas tend to have children with stronger literacy skills. On the other hand, families characterized by drug, alcohol, or psychological problems, and lack either reading material or educational activities at home, are more likely to have children with weaker literacy skills.

Family context is an important consideration for children's emerging literacy skills. Not only do children acquire basic language skills within their families but much of their learning takes place in the early years before children enter formal education (Purcell-Gates, 1993). Parents who have poor literacy themselves are seriously limited in their ability to facilitate their children's literacy learning, and have a difficult time passing on positive attitudes about the importance of learning, school, and reading (Newman & Beverstock, 1990; Smith, 1984).

Resiliency factors that protect against poor literacy are emerging from research findings. For example, the connection between early experiences with books and later success with reading has been established (Parker, 1989). Also, training parents to teach literacy skills to their children has resulted in positive effects for children's language skills (Whitehurst and colleagues, 1994). Moreover, training parents in this way appears to have a stronger impact on children's literacy progress than providing the same training to schoolteachers (Valdez-Menchaca & Whitehurst, 1992).

Intervention efforts to combat illiteracy and poor literacy largely take the form of literacy programs, and it is through the evaluation of such programs that we learn whether literacy interventions are successful or not. The current trend in evaluation of literacy programs is against uniformity of measurement, and instead calls for tailoring evaluation to the local needs of programs (Ryan, Geissler, & Knell, 1996). The major advantage of "localizing" evaluation is the opportunity to involve program staff in monitoring of their own services. The major disadvantage, of course, is that evaluation results are not easily compared across programs.

The purpose of this study was to evaluate client outcomes of a rural literacy program during its pilot year of operation. The major impetus for evaluation was to gather data to inform program development.

THE PROGRAM

The Home Based Literacy program was designed to provide services to rural families in communities where no other literacy services were available. The program's two main objectives were: (1) to increase children's literacy skills and (2) to increase parent's abilities to increase their children's literacy skills. Program services were designed to include twenty 15-minute sessions that were provided to families in their own homes. Specifically, workers visited family homes on 20 occasions over 4 weeks. On each occasion, the worker spent 15 minutes initiating and engaging parents and their children in activities that were tailored to address unique family and literacy needs.

The most common activities were modeling reading with children, listening to parent concerns, pointing out parent strengths in relation to helping their children, and teaching literacy games. Parents were expected to continue the activity or follow through later in the day after the worker's departure. The rationale behind such short but frequent sessions was to establish daily literacy habits in family households.

As it happened, two-thirds of all families actually received the program as it was originally designed (i.e., 20 sessions of 15 minutes each) during the pilot year of operation. Program modifications were made in response to practical considerations that arose during implementation. For example, travel time to some rural families took 3 to 4 longer than the time of one 15-minute session. For these "long-distance" families, adjustments were made so that the duration of each in-home session at least equaled the length of travel time. A worker staying 45 minutes, for example, counted one visit as three sessions. Overall, the feasibility of the program's design was supported by the fact that less than 20 percent of families canceled (or did not show) for scheduled sessions.

METHOD

A one-group pretest-posttest design was used to evaluate the program. A limitation of this design is the inability to rule out the possibility that events other than the interventions of the literacy program affected client outcomes. A second noteworthy limitation is that the very act of taking a pretest may have sensitized parents to ways in which they could affect their children's literacy levels.

Sample

In the pilot year of the program, a total of 86 families received services, however, not all families provided all data requested for the evaluation. Missing data ranged from 7 to 22 percent across variables, which has negative consequences for generalizing study findings to all program recipients. This is particularly the case because the reasons for missing data are not known.

Based on the responses of 70 families, the two major referral sources for the program were local schools (53%) and self-referrals (40%). Over two-thirds (68%) of 69 families lived in one of nine rural townships served by the program. The remaining one-third of families lived in outlying farmland areas. Of 83 families who provided data on race, most were Caucasian (83%) and spoke English as their first language. Minority families served included Arabic, Chinese, East Indian, Japanese, Mexican, and Native American. The average number of children per family was 3 and the range was 1 to 5.

Sixty-six of 70 families (94%) reported that mothers were the primary adult program participants, taking responsibility for meeting literacy workers and working with their child(ren) during sessions. The high rate of participation by mothers can, in part, be explained by the fact that fewer mothers (57%, $n = 77$) were employed outside the home, as compared to fathers (95%, $n = 65$).

Most parents were 26 years and older. Mothers and fathers were similar in achieved years of education, with a median of grade 12 in both groups. The ranges for years of education were 5 to 18 years for mothers and 3 to 18 years for fathers. Just over half (57%) of 83 families said they had a current library card.

Data Collection

Data were collected using an unstandardized questionnaire that was developed by program staff in an effort to ensure that the measuring instrument would target the specific objectives of the program. The questionnaire had parents rate how often they engaged in 13 literacy-related activities with their children. The following 6-point scale was used to rate each activity: 1 = everyday, 2 = about every other day, 3 = once or twice a week, 4 = several times a month, 5 = once a month or less, and 6 = never.

Table G-1   Changes in Parent Behaviors ($N = 73$)

Parent Behaviors	Program Start		Program Exit			
How often do you....	M_S	SD	M_E	SD	$M_S - M_E$	$p*$
Listen to your child read	2.6	1.6	1.7	1.0	.9	.01
Talk about pictures/words in a story	2.4	1.3	2.0	0.9	.4	.05
Read to your child	2.2	1.4	1.8	1.2	.4	.05
Sing songs to your child	3.2	1.7	3.0	1.8	.2	ns
Talk about a TV show together	2.8	1.7	3.0	1.7	-.2	ns
Look at books or magazines together	2.2	1.3	2.4	1.3	-.2	ns
Cook or bake with your child	3.4	3.0	3.6	1.4	-.2	ns
Play a game (cards, board games, etc.)	3.6	1.3	3.4	1.5	.2	ns
Help your child write a card/letter	3.8	1.6	4.0	1.4	-.2	ns
Go grocery shopping with your child	3.6	1.2	3.7	1.1	-.1	ns
Watch TV together	2.3	1.4	2.4	1.5	-.1	ns
Tell stories to your child	3.1	1.6	3.1	1.4		ns
Talk about school with your child	1.3	1.0	1.4	1.0	-.1	ns

*p is based on correlated t-test

Program staff decided to forgo the benefits of a standardized questionnaire because the primary intent of the evaluation was to collect data for program development purposes and not to make comparisons with other programs. As a result, the questionnaire used had high face validity and considerable value for informing program development decisions.

RESULTS

Table G-1 presents the changes in frequency of literacy related activities made by parents from the beginning to the end of the program. In short, parents engaged in the following activities more often: listened to their children read, talked about pictures/words in a story, and read to their children. While the increase for all three of these activities was statistically significant, the absence of a control group in the research design precludes any conclusions that the improvements were caused by the program.

In addition to showing a statistically significant increase in frequency for the top three listed activities, Table G-1 also shows that there was less variation at posttest. In other words, by the end of the program fewer parents reported extremely low occurrences for these activities. For example, at pretest 11 parents reported that they listen to their child read only once a month or less, or never. At posttest, only one parent reported in the never category.

Although none of the negative difference scores in Table 1 were statistically significant, the results are promising in that they show decreases in frequency of activities that *indirectly* relate prose literacy development (i.e., looking at books or magazines) and increases in frequency of activities that *directly* related to prose literacy development (i.e., reading to children). Since families are naturally limited in the number of activities they can engage in per day, the exchange of indirect literacy activities for direct ones seems a positive trade-off.

DISCUSSION AND IMPLICATIONS

The evaluation findings indicated that parents significantly increased the amount of time spent listening to their children read, talking about pictures or words in a story, and reading to their children by the end of the program. These outcomes are particularly encouraging since less than 40 percent of Canadians and Americans report that they read books daily (OECD and Statistics Canada, 1995). Also promising was the fact that families reduced the amount of time spent watching television, which can interfere with family literacy. Watching television not only occupies time that could be spent on reading but it also provides easy access to information, which reduces the need to read (OECD and Statistics Canada, 1995). As such, television watching may be counter-productive to literacy development.

The increase in frequency of literacy-related activities within families not only lends support to home-based family-centered literacy programs, it also supports the reasons to justify family literacy programs in general, as identified by Sharon Skage (1997). First, parents do not often realize how much influence they have on their children's literacy development. Second, parents with low literacy skills or poor attitudes toward literacy can negatively affect their children's literacy development. Third, parents' need support to develop their self-confidence in tackling the job of being their children's first teachers. Fourth, parents with low literacy skills need support to take on an active role with their children's school. Fifth, parents and caregivers can be more easily motivated to participate in family literacy programs as compared to adult-only literacy programs. Finally, family literacy has positive implications for family relationships.

The positive changes reported by parents at the end of the program ought to be considered in the context of how the program was actually implemented. Specifically, it is important to acknowledge that the original literacy program design was not fully implemented given that adjustments were made to increase the duration of sessions but reduce the number of worker visits for some rural families who lived more than one-half hour away from the program.

Further study is needed to directly compare the outcomes of families who receive different variations of program services. Given that the Home-Based Literacy program was in its early stages of development, any comparisons to other literacy programs must be made with caution. Specifically, programs in start-up mode tend to experience greater change, making program services unstable for comparison purposes.

As discussed earlier, there is a strong relationship between illiteracy and poverty. Improvement in literacy is linked to success of individuals in society in terms of achieving self-sufficiency. Parents who recognize the significant role they play in helping their children achieve literacy can also impact their children's literacy learning. Home-based literacy programs such as the one reported on in this study empower parents to provide their children with the literacy tools needed to achieve self-sufficiency in a rapidly changing world.

Moreover, such programs also provide parents more opportunities to achieve positive and fulfilling interaction with their children, which can lead to stronger relationships. Given the potential for promoting stronger family relationships and self-sufficiency, support for family focused, home-based literacy programs should rank high among the kinds of efforts supported by the social work community.

REFERENCES

Bishop, M. (1991), Why Johnny's dad can't read: The elusive goal of universal adult literacy. *Policy Review, 55,* 19-25.

Cronan, T.A., Cruz, S.G., & Arriaga, R.I. (1996). The effects of a community-based literacy program on young children's language and conceptual development. *American Journal of Community Psychology, 24,* 251-272.

Newman, A.P., & Beverstock. (1990). *Adult literacy: Contexts and challenges.* Newark, DE: International Reading Association.

Organization for Economic Co-operation and Development - OECD (1995). *Literacy, economy, and society: Results of the first international adult literacy survey.* Ottawa, Ontario: Statistics Canada.

Parker, J.M. (1989). Building bridges in midtown Manhattan: An intergenerational literacy program. *Urban Education, 24*, 109-115.

Purcell-Gates, V. (1993). Issues for family literacy: Voices from the trenches. *Language Arts, 70*, 670-677.

Ryan, K. E., Geissler, B., & Knell, S. (1996). Progress and accountability in family literacy: Lessons from a collaborative approach. *Education and Program Planning, 19*, 263-272.

Skage, S. (1997). *Guide to evaluation for family literacy projects in Alberta*. Brooks, Alberta: Family Literacy Action Group of Alberta.

Smith, F. (1984). The creative achievement of literacy. In H. Goelman, A. Oberg, & F. Smith (Eds.), *Awakening to literacy: The University of Victoria symposium of children's response to literacy environments*. Portsmouth, NH: Heinemann Educational Books.

Valdez-Menshaca, M.C., & Whitehurst, G.J. (1992). Accelerating language development through picture book reading: A systematic extension to a Mexican daycare. *Developmental Psychology, 28*, 1106-1114.

Whitehurst, G.J., Arnold, D.S., Epstein, J.N., Angell, A.L., Smith, M., & Fischel, J.E. (1994). A picture book reading intervention in day care and home for children from low-income families. *Developmental Psychology, 30*, 679-689.